TORTOISE QUARTERLY | EDITION 2

MOTHERLAND

Tortoise Media
16–19 Eastcastle Street
London W1W 8DY

Copyright © Tortoise Media 2019

ISBN 978-1-913323-04-2

Typeset in 10.7 / 12.5pt
Wolpe Pegasus

All photographs by Getty Images
unless credited

Design by Jon Hill

Repro by DawkinsColour

Printed by Pureprint, a Carbon
Neutral® Company, on an FSC®
certified paper from responsible
sources. The paper is Carbon
Balanced with the World Land Trust,
an international conservation charity
who offset carbon emissions through
the purchase of high conservation
value land.

WORLD
LAND
TRUST™
www.carbonbalancedpaper.com
CBP00019082564163028

www.tortoisemedia.com

On the cover:
Melting Landscapes by
Fernando Moleres
See page 128

With thanks to:
Christian Edwards
David Edwards
Imogen Harper
Michelle Henderson
Jon Jones
Joe Mee
Liz Moseley
Chris Newell
Ellie Pogrund
Annabel Shepherd-Barron

Contents

"I know you have a little life in you yet,
I know you have a lot of strength left"

This Woman's Work by Kate Bush, 1988

A note from the editor of this book

Welcome to the second edition of the Tortoise Quarterly short book of long reads. Our loose theme is parenting: our cover and photo essay pay mournful tribute to the mother of us all: Earth, our melting world. Catherine Nixey takes narrower aim: she was seven months pregnant when she delivered her essay on the way we talk about maternity.

Tortoise readers will be familiar with the dreadful story of Daphne Caruana Galizia, murdered in Malta by persons unknown (some say) two years ago. Her son Paul returned to the island for the first time since his mother's death and found his meditations there turning towards his father. And on the subject of fatherhood, the fact that my father, had he lived, would have been a hundred this month, seemed an opportunity for me to put something right.

It's not all about parenting, though. Jonathan Cake's account of playing Coriolanus in New York this summer is about much more than the actor's lot. Martin Samuel, perhaps the most influential sports journalist in the UK, considers the career of Gary Lineker, a fine footballer turned political player. And the mighty Edith continues her adventures with the latest instalment of Millennial Living.

Lastly, a word for one of our members, Susie Walker, whose brilliant account of following the hard road to becoming a female stand-up comic is a reminder that you, the Tortoise collective, are our best source of inspiration.

As previously, none of the good things here could have been achieved without Imogen Harper. ◠.

Keith Blackmore, *Editor*

Motherland

Why don't we talk truthfully about childbirth? An expectant Catherine Nixey wants to know

Vaginas are not the Bible's strong suit. Which is odd, in a way, as this is a book obsessed by birth. The Bible begins with a birth (of sorts) – of man. It abounds in "begats". And it contains what is probably the most famous birth – if not the most famous scene of all – in western literature: the birth of Jesus. But it is all notably light on vaginas. Or rather the version of it that we happen to have is.

As I approach the birth of my third child, this is very much on my mind. History is full of "what ifs". What if Hitler had won the Second World War? What if Napoleon hadn't been defeated at Waterloo? What if John had never met Yoko? To these well-known chances I would suggest that one more should be added: what if the heretical book known as the Infancy Gospel of James had been included in the Bible?

This is not, admittedly, a "what if" that will stir many hearts. Most people haven't heard of this gospel today. Unsurprisingly: the early church banned it to ensure just that. But had this gospel been accepted it might have changed the way that we looked not only at the Virgin Mary but also at the entirety of womankind for the past 2,000 years. It would certainly have changed the way we look at vaginas.

For unlike the better known gospels, which skip discreetly over the birth of Jesus in a few brisk words, this one lingers. Mary feels the contractions begin. A midwife is sought and found. There is drama, and delivery. And then comes one of the oddest scenes in biblical literature. After the birth an interfering woman, uninvited, inserts her hand into Mary's vagina. Whereupon Mary's violated vagina promptly burns the woman's hand to a crisp. Few women who have given birth could forbear to cheer. Mary, we are with you.

As birth looms, I think of this scene often. Not just because uninvited hands are approaching for me, too, though they are. As I write, I am about three weeks from my due date. Not long after typing this, I will almost certainly be in a hospital room and, if the last experiences are anything to go by, in the midst of unimaginable pain and inexcusable swearing. But the main reason I think of it is because, in literary history, it is an awesome rarity. For it is not just the Bible that is light on vaginas and birth. It is pretty much the entirety of the western canon.

Little else in life is so poorly covered. Like Ecclesiastes, literature has time for everything under the heavens. Whatever the life event, books and poems are there for you. Literature teaches us how to suffer war and enjoy peace; how to endure pride and face prejudice; how to meet with disaster and defeat. It teaches us how to live, and how to die: who doesn't know that they shouldn't go gentle into that good night but rage, rage against the dying of the light?

But when it comes not to dying but to giving birth? Silence. A great and resounding silence. We read to know we are not alone, wrote CS Lewis. But for childbirth and the odd, eerie, isolating days and months after there is almost nothing to read. And you will rarely feel so alone in your life. The Irish writer Anne Enright, one of the few who has written about this, once wondered why. "Can mothers not hold a pen?"

I blame the Virgin Mary. Women can hold pens – but over the centuries few have held with women holding those pens to write about this. Men have shown little more zest for the topic. The sizzling virgin vagina is a rare aberration. Most biblical accounts bounce over the birth of Jesus swiftly, without detail – and certainly without vaginas.

One might say: naturally. This is religious literature. It has no place for that sort of thing. Except it does. Or rather, it did. The Bible is full of penises – and not just in those endless discussions on circumcision and how the fashionable faithful are wearing them these days (long, or cropped fashionably short?). The Old Testament also contains, as the academic Francesca Stavrakopoulou points out in a new book, veiled but detailed descriptions of God's own (it's massive, naturally).

Other religious literature enjoys a nice vagina. Take this from a prayer of the ancient Sumerian goddess

Inanna: "My untilled land lies fallow…. / Who will plow my vulva?/ Who will plow my high field? /Who will plow my wet ground?" And so on. What a different tone would be struck by *Carols from King's* if that popped up in one of the readings.

It wouldn't just be *Carols from King's* that would be changed. The whole of western literature might have taken a different turn if the Infancy Gospel of James had been included in the Bible. The Bible was the word of God and what was good enough for God was, on the whole, good enough for us. But the vagina, alas, was increasingly good enough for neither.

ary, already a virgin, became increasingly unsexed by later theologians. Not only, they argued, did she not have sex to produce Jesus. She never had sex afterwards either. Ever. The female eunuch was born, and ever after there has been a hole in western literature. Or more to the point, there hasn't. This, I think, affects us still.

Recently, someone asked me what birth was like. And to my horror I realised I didn't know. I have done it twice. I am about, I hope, to do it for a third time. And I can't describe it. I thought and thought, after I was asked, and found it all but impossible to put into words. This, I believe, is in large part due to the fact that I have almost never read any other writer putting it into words either.

It's not that there aren't books on birth – there are thousands of them, most with lettering in pink and baby blue. But these books are manuals, not literature. Literature and manuals fulfil entirely opposing functions:

manuals tell you about things you don't know, in bad prose; literature tells you about things you do, in good. People think of writing as creative and inventive but it isn't, really. The best writers don't cook things up. They boil things down. They form the unformed thought so we can hold and safely handle what is in our heads.

We experience things more clearly after we have read good literature on them. Going into a church will always feel different once you have read Larkin's *Church Going*. Slough feels more Sloughlike after Betjeman. Christmas is more Christmassy once you have read Dickens. But there has been no Larkin of the labour ward. As a result, I was entirely unprepared for what such a ward might be like.

This is absurd. If you had put me in the trenches of the First World War, I would be appalled but, I suspect, unsurprised. Primed by poetry, I would know what to expect: mud, blood, terror. From Wilfred Owen's *Dulce et Decorum Est* I would have expected the thick green light of a chlorine attack. From Siegfried Sassoon's *Glory of Women* I would have known that injured soldiers were welcomed home more warmly if "wounded in a mentionable place".

Yet for childbirth I was clueless. This is not to equate childbirth and war. But it is worth considering that in the modern western world in peacetime you are unlikely to experience sudden blood or pain, or the agony of unanaesthetized wounds or the risk of sudden trauma and death – unless, that is, you give birth. Yes, unlike war, childbirth usually ends well. But nonetheless it's still fairly dramatic along the way.

I'm not alone in being unaware. Megan Stack, a war correspondent who was unfazed by reporting on terrorism but knocked sideways by childbirth, has written lucidly about the experience of having a baby. In an interview she said she "really was unprepared for a lot of the things that happened that first year... even the simple biological facts [of] pregnancy and delivery of the baby". Stack was an educated, intelligent woman but to her this was "all shocking".

War is a star of stage and screen, garlanded with books, ceremonies, films, statues, poems, days of national celebration... Childbirth, on the other hand, which produces all those boys who are sent off to be slaughtered, gets almost nothing. Barely a mention.

Look up "war" in the *Oxford Dictionary of Quotations* and you will find 190 entries, ranging from Shakespeare ("Let slip the dogs of w.") to the modern day. "Childbirth" by contrast, has one, sole, solitary entry. It is outstripped in significance not only by "war" but also by "cherries" (nine entries including "American as c. pie") and "chickens" (eight).

What little literature does exist on birth itself is mainly medical and often antiquated, smelling of carbolic acid and condescension. A woman who loses her baby might find herself told that it is because she has an "incompetent cervix". Women whose babies fail to put on weight, as one of mine did, find their child damned by the regency sounding complaint of "failure to thrive". Floral metaphors reward more successful women, who might learn that their cervixes are "ripening" or they themselves are "blooming".

The tone of much else is one of artificial jollity. As you stand on the threshold of the nursery you discover that, linguistically, you're already in it. Midwives chummily call you "Mum". Not "a mum". Or "the mum". Just "Mum"; an abrupt shearing of self that shocked me the first time it happened. The baby was not yet out and already the me I knew, the "Catherine" I thought I was, had gone. "Mum" was there in her place.

Childbirth isn't all glum. There is, on the bright side, gas and air. In hospitals, this mixture of nitrous oxide and oxygen is called Entonox, which makes it sound suitably solemn and medical. It's not. It's marvellous. It is also one of the rare moments in childbirth that has a literary history. Nitrous oxide was hugely in vogue among the Victorians and William James, the psychologist and brother of Henry, described the experience of a man who used to take it. As Bertrand Russell records in his *History of Western Philosophy*: "Whenever he was under its influence, he knew the secret of the universe, but when he came to, he had forgotten it. At last, with immense effort, he wrote down the secret before the vision had faded. When completely recovered, he rushed to see what he had written. It was: 'A smell of petroleum prevails throughout.'"

It's a perfect description. While I was on gas and air I felt a similar omniscience. In the course of labour I shared my thoughts on everything from William James (a splendid fellow) to the health service in Peru (ropey) to the art on the walls of the hospital (even worse) with anyone who wanted to listen, and many who didn't.

But, on the whole, childbirth wasn't that much fun.

For my first baby I was put in a small ward room with one other smiling Eastern European woman, belly distended by her baby. She made friendly conversation with me between my trips to go and vomit in the toilet from the pain of my contractions. It is your first, she asked? Yes, I said, before going back to the toilet as another one struck. What are you having, she asked when I returned. A boy, I said. And you, I asked, when I came back. My baby is dead, she said. I am waiting to give birth to it. I returned to vomiting in the toilet.

or did I expect the pain. Before I gave birth I spoke to an Irish Catholic woman who had had four children and not screamed during any of the births. "Why would you scream?" she said. Having done it twice, I would suggest a better question is: why wouldn't you? You swear if you stub your toe. If someone tore off your toe (an injury closer to the tearing of childbirth) you'd surely have something to say about it.

To give you an idea of what must happen to your flesh, the average opening of the cervix before birth is narrower than the word "cervix" when written in this font size. The average baby's head, by contrast, is 35cm in circumference. You can see that something is going to have to give, and it isn't the baby.

During my second birth I felt less that I was in pain than that I was pain. A dazzling column of pain with no me left. Yet absurdly there is pressure, often from movements begun by men, for women to endure all this in silence and without pain relief because birth is "natural". So too is appendicitis, but there are fewer men calling for that to be endured in silence without pain relief.

One friend, stoic, sensible, suffered symptoms of PTSD after the birth of her first child; one experienced hair loss. Incontinence, at least for a short time, is routine. More severe incontinence is common. One friend came close to double incontinence. But, unlike Sassoon's soldiers, these women have been wounded in unmentionable places. So they won't discuss their injuries, except with close friends. What new mother has not sat, pale faced with pain, while relatives fuss round, unable to tell them to all go away, because to do so would be to admit publicly to not just having a vagina but, worse, that it hurts.

ere hours after the birth of Prince George, Kate Middleton stood on the steps of the Lindo Wing. Bump deflating slightly under her baby blue dress, her hair was perfect, her smile plucky. She didn't waddle, or wince. Dulce et decorum. You could barely have guessed, to look at her, that she was the new possessor of a body that must already have seemed alien and ungovernable. A body that, like a carcass in an abattoir, has suddenly had the life that was in it torn from it and that, newly hollowed out, will drip blood wherever it goes for weeks.

But things are, perhaps, changing. Meghan Markle, by appearing not hours but a defiant two days later, resolutely and charmingly un-soigne, made Middleton look slightly absurd: an island of archaism in a rising tide of feminism. Poor Kate, by always doing the right thing, now seems to have done the wrong one. Others are chipping away at the Middleton method too. The actress Keira Knightley recently wrote an essay about the birth of her first child that had little of the Lindo Wing about it. "My vagina split," she writes. "I remember the shit, the vomit, the blood, the stitches." She too was struck by what Middleton had to do. "Hide. Hide our pain, our bodies splitting, our breasts leaking, our hormones raging. Look beautiful, look stylish, don't show your battleground, Kate. Seven hours after your fight with life and death, seven hours after your body breaks open, and bloody, screaming life comes out. Don't show. Don't tell. Stand there with your girl and be shot by a pack of male photographers."

People like Knightley and Enright and Stack are starting to change these old attitudes. Writing about birth and childrearing is appearing that is brave and unashamed and good. Childbirth is still a topic without a literary history, without a past, but it, at least, is starting to gain a literary present; a presence. And when enough has been written perhaps we will see fewer books adorned with baby pink lettering. Fewer women made to stand on the steps of the Lindo Wing and smile. Fewer people who believe the old lies. ●.

From the author: Christopher Whipple was born on 18 September 2019, weighing 7lb 7oz, with very little fuss and quite a lot of gas and air.

He had left Malta and his father just hours after the funeral of his murdered mother and not been back since

Will you come home now?

By Paul Caruana Galizia

I t is a warm April night. My plane touches down. It would be better to be anywhere than here.

My father had been asking me to come home for a year and a half. "You're being funny about it," he'd say. "You can't avoid Malta for ever, you know."

So I gave in. But my uneasiness in the Gatwick departure lounge turned into an almost physical sense of dread as flight 8825 took off.

I did not think my heart could bear it. Then, when somewhere over Italy the plane began to shake, I thought: Jesus, this is all I need.

Why had I listened to him? Jessica, my wife, had the right idea: we have spent enough time in Malta, she said. It's taken enough.

It's a short flight, I had told her to reassure myself. We'll still feel like we're in London when we get there. We'll arrive quickly, leave quickly.

I used to go back to Malta often. So often that my connection to the place felt weaker. Often enough that, year after year, Malta came to mean less to me.

But now, stepping on to the tarmac, all my memories rush to meet me. The heaviness in the air, the limestone terminal and its inverted arches and, inside, the glistening tiles and smell of detergent. By the time I walk out of the terminal I feel tired, as though I have come a much greater distance than the 1,300 miles from London.

Matthew, the eldest and wildest brother, is waiting for me in the car park. Unbelievable. After all this time – all those pleas that I should come, and that flight, all that dread – my father isn't there to meet me. He has sent Matthew instead and a typically abrupt text: "At school reunion. See you at home."

Still, I am happy to see Matthew and, in a way, relieved. My father's driving is calm and safe, but also nauseating: corners taken with wide swerves; hills with stop-start acceleration.

My father had picked me up the last time I landed in Malta. Matthew in the front seat and Andrew, my middle brother, with me in the back. I remember now how desperate I was to feel as though nothing had happened. I remember exchanging glances with Andrew as we swerved down the familiar road to our house in Bidnija.

In 1990 we had moved from Sliema to Bidnija, a hamlet that sits on a ridge separating two valleys in the less arid north-west of Malta. No more than a half-hour drive to the urban core around Valletta on the north coast, people always asked why we lived so far away.

Buses came late to Bidnija, and taxi drivers often refused to go there. I once got a taxi home by telling the driver I needed to go to Mosta, a large town five minutes away. When at the edge of Mosta I asked the driver to please keep going, just a little bit, down

The spot near the family home in Bidnija where Daphne Caruana Galizia was murdered by a car bomb in October 2017. Previous page: Paul's father Peter the hill to our house, he said "ħxejtni, sieħbi, hawnhekk mhux Mosta" (you screwed me, friend, this isn't Mosta) and demanded an extra half-fare.

Broke, I got out halfway down the hill, not far from the field that now, as we drive past it, I see is full of flowers, candles, and a banner with my mother's portrait on it.

Matthew and I fall silent as we see the banner. We don't speak again until we reach our house.

This is the most painful thought for me: my brother, who ran out barefoot to the scene that day, driving past that banner each time he leaves and returns home, determined to look ahead but unable to look away.

The land is rugged, presenting plenty of opportunities for hideouts. The views from our house are wide. To the north, is the sea at St Paul's Bay, where we like to say our patron saint was shipwrecked on his way from Galilee to his execution in Rome. The old, fortified capital Mdina to the south and, looking west into the valley that opens up under the house, fields and an ancient olive grove.

The Bidni olive, a purple and alkaline cultivar, has grown in this valley for thousands of years and gave its name and purpose to our hamlet. Farmers built their farmhouses around the valley and by 1920 saved enough for a chapel that they dedicated to the Holy Family.

And that, really, is all. It is in this lonely hamlet that my parents decided we would settle, in a dilapidated house surrounded by a garden of citrus trees, bamboo and a mulberry tree that I can still see from my old room. Once that tree was home to migrating turtle doves; they were shot down by Maltese hunters.

My room. At last my room. I take off my jacket and throw it on to my desk, the same desk that had been mine since I was ten. It is covered with my stuff, some new, some old. A box with the Rizlas my parents never found, the books they gave me two Christmases ago.

Here I am again: the teenager, the 30-year-old, the boy, all at once. A text message from Andrew asks whether I'm home. Matthew brings my bag to my room. Both my brothers had come home months before me: the youngest and, as usual, the last.

Before closing the window shutters against the morning sun that will soon

The car bomb that killed Daphne left wreckage over a wide area, pictured above and on next page. The adjacent field (opposite) is now full of flowers and candles arrive, I look out across the dark to the coast, illuminated still by hotels, cars and houses, against a black sea.

Floating out there on his boat, a man once looked right back at this house and sent the signal that armed then detonated the bomb under my mother's car seat.

Malta has long been a place of violence, but the period of Labour rule, starting in 1971 and ending in 1987, a year before I was born, saw the country increasingly violent, isolated and divided.

Police raided the homes of people considered to be enemies of the state. The government expropriated their houses and businesses. Some left the country and never returned. But the eighties also saw thousands of people rise up in protest. They were met with brutality from the armed forces and police force, my father being one of many who was floored by a thug and beaten by policemen when the government ordered a crackdown on a protest in Valletta.

Government thugs burnt down the printing press of the *Times* and *The Sunday Times of Malta*, locking its workers inside the building. The workers escaped only with the help of a priest; the Church was then also an enemy of the state.

People were scared to express their views in private conversation let alone in print. Newspapers never carried bylines, columns were anonymous, reports always by "staff reporters".

Daphne, my mother, was politicised in this period. She was first arrested, aged 19, in 1984, at an anti-government protest. She was locked in a cell with faeces-covered walls and without access to the outside world for 24 hours. They tried forcing her to sign a false confession.

It was in 1987 that, by a whisker, a new party was voted into government on a platform of unity and modernisation. But the post-1987 reconciliation was a sham; no one paid for the crimes they had committed. The man who arrested my mother is now the speaker of our parliament. He sent flowers to her funeral the last time I was home.

For most Maltese people, the culture of fear still prevails. Why stick your neck out? What do you stand to gain? The violence of the 1980s is now washed away with platitudes (it was a different time) or, increasingly, revisionism (Labour's golden age).

The Great Siege monument in Valletta has served as a memorial to Daphne, with tributes left to honour her and demand that justice is done

More than 30 years after these events, Malta has still not had a proper accounting of that period. Worse, we think we don't need one. We bury our bodies with what we have: hyper-growth, powered by mass tourism, gambling and illicit finance.

And still we pay: corrupt politicians remain with us while the prize has grown with our economy; we have become a democratic country but an anti-democratic people; and high-profile murders still go unsolved.

And so in Malta people are asked to live in two worlds at once: daylight bombings and easy money. In a small country, you learn to live with anything.

I t was Matthew who last called me back to Malta. He rang from a number I didn't recognise. I sent the number to my mother, asking whether she knew it. No answer. And so when I finally picked up, he said that there was a bomb in her car and that he didn't think she made it and will you come home? Will you come home now? he said.

For the following three weeks we were under siege. The Bidnija valley we knew so well was lit at night by floodlights and in the day dotted with officers in white forensic suits. Drones buzzed overhead and questions from police officers, journalists, the president, all their questions and calls, flew around us. I left a few hours after the funeral and told myself I'd never return.

Waking up early in my old room, I lie in bed until my father opens the door and then knocks. "You can't stay in bed for ever, you know." Why not? "I suppose you can, but your brother wants to go swimming."

My father is lowering himself into the driver's seat when Matthew calls out behind him: "I'll drive – don't worry – I'll drive."

We drive to the coast south of Bidnija, a part rugged enough to keep the crowds away. It wasn't always like this. I remember being among a handful of people at the beach when we first moved to the area, but now the population has doubled and people drive all over the island looking for some sliver of uncrowded coast.

We walk down clay hills, moving through spring's clover and thyme, to get to the shore. The work makes us feel good; our peace

Daphne holding her eldest son Matthew in 1989.

deserved. We sit on a limestone slab jutting out into the sea, the sun slowly burning overhead. The heat comes early to Malta, but the sea this April day is still cold and rough. The waves overtake each other, one breaking after the other. Behind them the swell is like a body breathing.

Matthew jumps in. "It's perfect."

My father takes a step back from the shore, folds his arms behind his back in his usual way, and looks out at the waves crashing beside him. What is he thinking? His eyes fixed on the waves, what is my father thinking? The last time I felt like this I was nine years old, sitting on the sandy beach one headland south along the coast, watching my brothers swim and waiting for our parents to take us home. Home to tea and peaches so ripe that they melt in your hands as you peel them. It feels for a moment that nothing has happened in between. That moment is beautiful.

My father walks back to the limestone shore, arms still folded behind his back, the waves still rolling in out of the swelling grey sea, saying to him in a way that his sons can't that things go on. ◖.

Above:
Peter with
Andrew (left)
and Paul.

Opposite:
Daphne
celebrates her
24th birthday

He's the Remain star of Brexit and the BBC's highest-paid presenter. Oh, and he could play a bit in his day too. Gary Lineker is still hitting the target

The political footballer

By Martin Samuel

Gary Lineker's new book contains a recipe for asparagus risotto, but it's not a cookbook. It contains personal anecdotes and stories, too, but nor is it an autobiography. It's the literary cash-in on a very listenable podcast he hosts with the outstanding broadcaster Danny Baker. It is well known to listeners that the show is recorded at Lineker's home, and that he cooks each week for the crew. So now there is an appetite for Lineker's take on Italian vegetarian staples, as well as his view on Manchester City's defensive formation, Steve Smith's batting, Brexit, or anything, really.

There's a bit of a myth about risotto, too. A lot of home cooks will say it's hard to master, but it isn't. It's comparatively formulaic. It begins with a sofrito base of onion and garlic, maybe celery; there will be a stage in which the main ingredient is added, wine to deglaze the pan, rice, then stock, poured in gradually ladle by ladle until al dente; finally butter and parmesan cheese giving a creamy finish. For asparagus risotto, it is best to cook the stems for longer than the tips, which can be blanched and placed on top. Stems might be blended or broken down for a greener finish. Apologies if you already know this. Most competent cooks do.

And as Lineker is, by all accounts, a competent cook, his recipe will not differ greatly to the above. If it does, it really isn't asparagus risotto. Nevertheless, this mundane detail

Gary Lineker: a man for all seasons	1960 Born 30 November in Leicester, the eldest son of a greengrocer.	1977 Joins Leicester City straight from school. Makes his debut two years later, aged 18.	1982 Finishes Division Two season with 19 goals, helping Leicester reach the FA Cup semi-final.

goes to make a page in his book. Because people aren't really interested in asparagus risotto; they're interested in Gary Lineker's Asparagus Risotto – much as their attention is captured by Reese Witherspoon's Fried Chicken or Gwyneth Paltrow's Butternut Squash Tacos.

Just as he was as a footballer, Lineker is now the consummate performer on his chosen stage. He negotiates his way through modern media and celebrity as expertly as he judged his runs in the shirts of Leicester, Everton, Barcelona, Tottenham or England. Better, in fact, because with age has come a certain understanding of his place in the world and wisdom on how to remain there.

Lineker's intuition as a footballer was natural. His post-playing career needed more work, but Lineker knows who he is, and what he is about now. Footballers always receive and demand coaching, until the day they retire. Lineker, 59 in November, no longer requires steering by a superior. He is a slyly witty presence in the television studio and on social media, a sometimes outspoken political influencer and one of the most instantly recognisable faces in Britain today. Those who do not remember him as an exceptionally gifted goalscorer know him as the long-standing presenter of *Match of the Day* and mischievous huckster for Walkers crisps, where he plays the inverse of his old goody-two-shoes persona. Not that he wears the halo any more, now

1985
Scores 24 goals in Division One to be joint top scorer. Earns an £800,000 move to champions Everton.

1985
Wins the Charity Shield in his first proper game for Everton, beating Manchester United at Wembley.

the world has been introduced to the politicised, sweary, call-it-as-you-see-it Lineker on Twitter.

It began with a humanitarian defence of refugees, at a time when the fashion was for demonisation for political ends. The backlash to this – *The Sun* abandoned the standard of free speech and called for his dismissal, as did several Conservative MPs – has if anything been emboldening. "Whatever the result, Farage will always be a dick," he tweeted around the time of the referendum in 2016.

And, no, this is hardly revelatory stuff, either. Farage has failed to win election to Parliament on seven occasions personally and his Brexit Party couldn't take Leave-voting Peterborough even when the incumbent Labour MP turned out to be a crook. He cosies up to Donald Trump and the alt-right and he used overtly racist tropes while campaigning to leave the European Union. Seriously, the engorged penis of Johnny Wadd, the legendary porn star, was not as much of a dick as Nigel Farage. So it's not that Lineker is saying much that is new. More that if he thinks Farage is a dick, it carries such greater cachet than, say, half the population agreeing.

It is this Lineker, and his status as the most prominent Remainer in Britain, that affords him such prominence in modern public life. At a time of extremes he is often the

1986
Enjoys a lighter moment with the Colorado police during England's World Cup preparations.

1986
Hits 40 goals in 57 games for Everton, who finish second in the league.

most influential embodiment of centrist reason. "I'd like to take it back three years and just eradicate everything," he told LBC, sorrowfully. "We've turned into such a hateful place, it's so sad." Amen to that.

Much like the risotto recipe, though, it is not so much what Lineker says, or does, that contains the secret to his success – more the identity of the person holding this opinion. Lineker isn't tweeting mind-blowing resolutions to the problems around the Irish backstop. Equally, his insights into Farage, or Boris Johnson, or Michael Gove, or Jacob Rees-Mogg are not unique, or even controversial, given there are probably tens of millions arguing the same in houses, public and private, across Britain. The power is not in what is being said, but in who is doing the saying. It's Gary Lineker. Gary Lineker says Nigel Farage is a dick. That's your headline right there.

Earlier this year he was accosted by an old woman at Euston Station, who pushed him in the back, swearing and shouting that he would let Isis bride Shamima Begum back in the country. "Fuck you. Fucking Lineker. You'd have her back, wouldn't you?" she ranted. Lineker says he was so surprised he didn't have time to answer properly, before she marched off to a rally in support of Tommy Robinson. Yet it encapsulates his status at the heart of British political life. Lineker is one of those people who have somehow

1987
His first season in Spain brings 20 goals in 41 games for Terry Venables's Barcelona

come to own Brexit and the issues around it. And he's had a very good Brexit. He's the Jacob Rees-Mogg of Remain. He's the breakout star. "I get a lot more hate than I've ever had in my life," he told the *Daily Mirror*, "but I get loads more love, too."

Lineker has 7.4m Twitter followers compared to 147,000 for Jo Swinson, leader of the Liberal Democrats party, or even 2.1m for Jeremy Corbyn, so his reach is greater than either of the opposition leaders. Politicians would kill for his influence, which is probably why he gets asked, and frequently, to head up fledgling centrist parties. The nearest he has come is as a prominent supporter of the campaign for a second referendum, People's Vote. Beyond that, Lineker says, he would hate a life in politics. "It would bore me senseless, shaking people's hands and holding babies," he told *The Times* this year. "I have no interest in that."

Part of the reason for this – aside from the fact he can make more lucrative use of his time – is it might hold Lineker, personally, up to awkward scrutiny. Not that he's a bad guy. But politicians, and increasingly those that involve themselves in political affairs, are expected to maintain very high standards. And Lineker has been a footballer, a media personality and spectacularly famous for a long time. That tends to make a person rather – whisper it – selfish.

1987
Settles into life in Spain with his wife Michelle and immediately learns Spanish. He becomes fluent.

Lineker's humanitarianism is sincere – it without doubt trumps any party political line, because he is an admitted swing voter – but, as witnessed first hand, he is also the sort of chap who puts his seat back on airplanes, even when flying short haul from football matches in Europe. And, no, it's not the crime of the century and plenty of people do it. However, it is one of those modern etiquette issues that are said to shine a light on character. Here's Debrett's on seat reclining. "This is a common bugbear. It's selfish to recline your seat during short daytime flights. When travelling by plane, always stay within your own designated space and don't hog the armrest." So what do we learn? That Lineker has led a somewhat privileged life as a professional footballer and television personality, and if preaching became his business, rather than a hobby, he might have a hard time living up to expectations.

And he's not alone in this. To digress briefly, consider Emma Thompson, whose role as a prominent supporter and voice for Extinction Rebellion went down about as well as her role as a dissident journalist in *Imagining Argentina*, a film described by *Guardian* critic Peter Bradshaw as "a cult classic of awfulness". Thompson flew 5,400 miles from Los Angeles to protest about climate change. Come on; you'd pay good money in the West End for irony as perfect as that. Don't laugh, though,

---

1988
Wins the Copa del Rey (the Spanish FA Cup) but then contracts hepatitis after Euro '88 finals.

1989
Wins European Cup-Winners' Cup with Barcelona. Signs for Tottenham for £1.1m and later admits that Sir Alex

Ferguson tried to sign him for Manchester United.

because she had a very good reason to be in LA. It was her birthday. So there. And it was all of two and a half weeks later when she was spotted boarding another long-haul flight at Heathrow Airport, despite returning to announce "we should fly less". "If I could fly cleanly, I would," said Thompson, which rather ignores option B, which is not flying at all. It's not exactly *The Remains of the Day* that Thompson has been jetting off to make of late, either. It's *Men in Black: International* – or Men in Black 4, if we're telling it as it is – a role that could just as necessarily be played by an actor living four blocks from the set, who could come to work on her bicycle. Honestly, we don't need a 3,000-tonne carbon footprint for *Cruella*, Emma. You stay home and protest. We'll get someone to come by on a scooter.

And if Lineker cops some of the liberal elite backlash, in the press and on social media, it's because he's perceived to be, like Thompson, a member of a privileged, distanced, media class that wants to hold others to standards it ignores when it suits. Lineker is also greatly troubled by green issues. This is what he had to say when asked to deliver his cod political manifesto to *The Times*. "The first thing I'd do is revoke Article 50. And then I think the most important thing on the planet is our planet." Wise words, mate, as Smashie and Nicey would note. Yet here's the

1990
Tops the Division One scoring charts for the third time with 24 league goals. Then helps England to the semi-final at Italia 90 with four goals. Famously warns England manager Bobby Robson to "keep an eye" on the tearful Gazza.

same man discussing his wealth and lifestyle choices with the *Financial Times*. "I don't crave to have billions and buy a yacht or any of that business, but I'd be lying if I didn't say I can have nice things. Money makes life easier. As long as I can eat where I want and have a nice holiday..." Judging by the tan, we can safely assume the nice holidays Lineker has in mind won't be taking place in a caravan near Skegness or in anything resembling a tent, with a side gamble on the British summer. So Lineker, like Thompson and many of the highest profile carers for the planet, are green right up until the moment it starts to impact on their choices. Put it like this: if Lineker asked Greta Thunberg, she'd no doubt rather he bought the yacht.

So what was Lineker like as a footballer? Where does he stand among England's goalscorers? Without doubt, one of the best. Greater than is remembered; better than his achievements show. Lineker is the proof that football is, above all, a results game because his personal record outweighs the successes of the clubs he played for, and of England at that time. Yet because his trophy cabinet is underwhelming, and does not include a major league title – just the FA Cup in England, and the Copa del Rey and European Cup-Winners' Cup with Barcelona – he is not afforded the same respect as many contemporaries. Tottenham do not consider him one of their own, unlike

1991
Wins FA Cup with Tottenham. *An Evening With Gary Lineker* opens at the Duchess Theatre.

Harry Kane, and Andy Gray, not Lineker, is the legend at 80s Everton. He missed the golden years at Barcelona, too, which leaves Leicester, his home town and greatest love, the club he still views as pessimistically as any fan – incapable of considering they could win the Premier League title in 2016, which is how he came to present *Match of the Day* in his underpants, after a flippant remark. Lineker played the majority of his games – 117 of 216 – for Leicester in the Second Division and was at Filbert Street for seven seasons, before moving to Everton the year after they won the title. There, he lasted a single season, yet his scoring record is magnificent: one every 1.36 matches. Gray, whose goals are considered to have powered Everton to the championship in the previous campaign, was good for a goal every 3.5 games. Yet Gray is recalled more fondly, for obvious reasons.

Lineker scored 41 goals in two seasons at Barcelona, before Johan Cruyff moved him to the wing, and even his final season at Tottenham was prolific, with 35 goals in 50 matches, before finishing his career as a trailblazer with Grampus Eight in Japan. For England, he was outstanding. Wayne Rooney broke his scoring record, yet Lineker remains the benchmark for England in tournaments (where Rooney disappointed, beyond the 2004 European Championship). Lineker was top scorer at the 1986 World

1992
Son George is born and spends many months in Great Ormond Street with leukaemia. Dad scores his final goal in English football on the last day of the season as Spurs lose at Old Trafford. Plays his final game for England, finishing with 48 goals from 80 games, one goal fewer than Bobby Charlton's record. Moves to Japan to play for Nagoya Grampus Eight.

Cup, and still holds England's record for goals scored in World Cup finals.

Technically, what set him apart was his reaction to the game, his runs, his timing, his anticipation. He was not a player who scored spectacular goals, or shot from range. If anything, he did not strike the ball as cleanly as contemporaries such as Clive Allen and often appeared to be losing his balance just at the moment the ball was hitting the net. Yet Lineker knew when to go; he had an innate sense of where he had to be in the penalty area and if his skills were not always the best, his instincts made up for that. And he scored goals in torrents, such as his three against Poland in 1986, or his hat-trick for Barcelona against Real Madrid in January 1987.

The footage of that Barcelona game can be found quite easily and tells the viewer all he needs to know about the man in the number nine shirt. For his first goal, Lineker makes an exquisitely judged run, in front of his marker, to convert a cross from Victor Muñoz, without the need for a second touch. The next goal, he is in the right place again at the far post, to pick up the rebound from a Carrasco shot. The third comes when he gambles, instinctively, that Madrid's central defence will not get to a long clearance by Barcelona goalkeeper Andoni Zubizarreta. Lineker makes his run – much as Luis Suárez did to score the winner for

1994
Ends his playing career aged 34 after scoring nine goals in 23 games in Japan. Has the staggering record of never receiving a yellow let alone a red card in more than 600 games.

1995
First Walkers crisps advert airs after signing a £200,000 deal. Appears on BBC's quiz show, *They Think It's All Over*.

1997
Presents *Grandstand*, one of the BBC's longest-running TV sports shows.

Uruguay against England at the 2014 World Cup – controls the ball cleanly and finishes bravely. There is nothing spectacular in this performance, nothing that would make the highlights reel for, say, a more artistic player from the same time like, say, Matt Le Tissier. Yet in every scene the native intelligence of a born matchwinner is visible. Barcelona win 3-2. It shows precisely, and succinctly, what Lineker brought to his teams.

And he was a smart player. Never booked, never sent off, but always aware of his surroundings. When Paul Gascoigne had his breakdown during the semi-final of the 1990 World Cup, it was Lineker who noticed first and brought it to the attention of Bobby Robson, the England manager. Gascoigne collected a second yellow card meaning he would miss the World Cup final if England got there. Emotionally fragile even then, he couldn't handle this possibility. His features crumble, tears begin to flow. Any one of his team-mates could have noticed this. Yet it fell to Lineker to signal the crisis to Robson. His gestures – recognisable as "keep an eye on him" – became one of the defining images of a match England would eventually lose. Later we think we see Robson consoling Gascoigne at the end of play – when those who were present claim he was actually desperately trying to persuade him to take a penalty – but it took Lineker to momentarily divorce

1999
Takes over from the great Des Lynam as presenter of *Match of the Day*.

himself from the match, and consider the wider issue unfolding. His managers say Lineker was an outstanding reader of the game. He might indeed have made a very good coach were it not for an aversion to one very important aspect of his sport.

Lineker was famously unenthusiastic about training – preferring a soak in a lukewarm bath and a little running – hiding behind the excuse that he did not want to use up his luck as a scorer, banging in goals cheaply for fun in practice. More likely, he was self-conscious about his scruffy Gerd Müller-like finishing. Terry Venables believed Lineker thought it would tarnish his mystique as the focal point of play if his team-mates saw his limitations striking the ball. When a goal is scored during a game, technique is immaterial. Who cares how it happens; everyone celebrates the scorer, few consider the method. Yet, in training, everyone is watching, and taking mental notes. Maybe Lineker didn't want it getting around that he had a weakness. Yet he wasn't lazy, and he was always alert to the play. And despite the angelic reputation and an unblemished disciplinary record, he was very capable of being one of the chaps.

Tottenham's dressing-room, in particular, was spiteful in its verbal exchanges and pranks, to the extent that Venables, the manager, was frequently appalled. "Nothing

2000
Walkers crisps TV ads are ranked ninth in Channel 4's poll of the 100 greatest adverts.

2002
Appears in the film *Bend it Like Beckham*.

in the Don Revie era had a glass eye, which the players used to persuade him to take out, and then hide. A coach driver at Liverpool was paid many times his salary – but nothing to the players – to drink a glass of fresh urine for the amusement of the team. Tottenham's gofer was John who, one day, was asked to fetch some kit from a roof-rack on top of a van, at which point Gascoigne jumped in and set off down the road, eventually turning on to the A1, which had to be taken at high speed. Had he been thrown off, John could have been killed. It probably seemed like fun at the time, much like shooting a pal with an air rifle for a laugh, which also happened at the training ground.

2002
Backs a £5m bid to rescue Leicester City, describing his involvement as "charity" rather than an "ego trip".

2003
Is inducted into English football's hall of fame at the National Football Museum.

2005
Becomes the BBC's new main golf presenter.

Yet Lineker moved as effortlessly through these child-like circles as he later would the button-down world of BBC broadcasting.

One incident in particular had Venables even more aghast than usual. Graham Taylor had succeeded Bobby Robson as England manager and brought his own coaches, including Steve Harrison, the type of assistant known as a players' man. Harrison was a good coach, but also had a personality capable of keeping the team happy, allowing the manager to be apart, and aloof. Not in the team? Moan to Steve. Need bucking up? Steve can make you smile. As well as coaching, it was Harrison's job to jolly the group along, to have a foot in each camp. To this end, he had a party trick. Rather an unusual one. Harrison's talent – if it could be termed so – was the ability to defecate into a paper cup, from a height – say, the top of a hotel room wardrobe. And no, it's hardly *The Marriage of Figaro*; but his chosen audience weren't first night at the Royal Opera House, either. Hearing stories of this, Venables seemed most disappointed with Lineker for finding it amusing. Venables had deliberately sought him out, seeking a like mind. "He said it was funny," Venables explained, shaking his head. "He said he makes a show of it, you know, spotlights, drum rolls…" Venables looked bemused. Lineker, he thought, should be above that.

2005
Harry Kewell sues for libel over Lineker's *Sunday Telegraph* column but the jury is unable to reach a verdict.

2006
Becomes the voice of *Underground Ernie*, the CBeebies series.

He and Michelle, mother of his four children, divorce after 20 years of marriage.

"Gary's one of the sensible ones," he mumbled, aghast.

The pair had a bond, having worked together at Barcelona and Tottenham. Venables admired the way Lineker and his then wife Michelle had immersed themselves in Catalan life, enjoying the culture, learning the language. Ian Rush moved to Juventus, failed to settle and famously described Italy as "like a foreign country" in an interview bemoaning the scarcity of baked beans in Turin. But Lineker was an enlightened soul, even then. He did not share the stereotypical insularity of British travellers in the 1980s. Venables – who was savvy enough to speak in Catalan, not Spanish, during his first public appearance at Nou Camp as Barcelona manager – was a kindred spirit in that sense, and the professional admiration was mutual. Lineker said that after he left Leicester, Venables was the only coach who taught him anything about goalscoring that he didn't know already. And this man worked with Johan Cruyff.

In broadcasting, Lineker was a quick learner, too. And from the best. At the BBC, he succeeded Des Lynam, a studio anchor so comfortable in his relationship with his audience that he opened the broadcast of the first match of England's 1998 World Cup campaign by looking directly into the camera as if peering personally into every home in the country. It was early Monday afternoon. Lynam

2009
Marries model Danielle Bux, who he met on a blind date in 2007.

didn't even bother with hello. "Shouldn't you be at work?" he asked, sardonically. It is the sort of quip one might imagine Lineker making now. Knowing, and witty, but with enough edge to be memorable. At the 1990 World Cup, Lineker's England team-mates were already mocking him as "Junior Des", because of his interest in the way journalism worked. He wrote his own columns, initially, for *The Sunday Telegraph* and is still proud that not much needed to be changed. One of the reasons he gives for never writing a proper autobiography is he wants the time to do the job himself.

Yet broadcast media was the best fit for Lineker's talents, and even if his first forays on to *Match of the Day* were unconvincing – ironically, the criticism was that his opinions were rather bland – he was smart enough to know that in Lynam there existed the perfect template for sports presenting. The ease, the casual charm, the effortless professionalism. If Lineker still has a penchant for hoary puns it is worth remembering that, unlike Lynam, he is not on his home field. Making the *Match of the Day* job his own, given who he succeeded, is a feat comparable to succeeding adequately Sir Alex Ferguson at Manchester United, which, so far, no manager has been able to do. We were discussing the Ferguson succession when I rather clumsily forgot his own circumstances. "You don't want to be the

2010
Resigns as a *Mail on Sunday* columnist in protest over the sting operation against FA chairman Lord Triesman.

Begins working as an anchor for Al Jazeera.

guy who follows Ferguson," I remarked. "You want to be the guy who follows the guy who follows Ferguson." "Yes, I must remember that," he replied, with a mocking eye roll. He hadn't long started his shift holding *Match of the Day* together but was already looking more at home in the role than David Moyes ever appeared at Manchester United. "I used to ask a lot of questions about the things Des did," Lineker recalled, "and picked up some of his nuances."

He certainly picked up Lynam's lightness of touch, which has allowed him to tiptoe through some heavily laid minefields, not least the row over his salary. When the BBC became obliged to document how much their star performers earned, Lineker turned out once again to be the centre-forward. He was the second highest, on £1.8m annually. Despite the fact that, undoubtedly, he could be paid even more to perform a similar role for Sky – his defence has always been that this is the "market rate" for his job – this was very easily juxtaposed with his status as bleeding-heart liberal and conscience of a nation. Against a backdrop of controversy over gender inequalities on pay, controversy on the use of national funds to finance extravagant salaries, for Mr Liberal Luvvie Elite Remainer to be top of the tree was a tap into an empty net for right-wing commentators. Get out of that, as Eric Morecambe would say.

2012
Gary Lineker's Football: It's Unbelievable! is published by Carlton Books.

But, deftly, Lineker did. "This whole BBC salary exposure business is an absolute outrage," he tweeted. "I mean, how can Chris Evans be on more than me?" And in one fell, 140-character swoop Lineker was free. He had acknowledged the issue, poked fun at himself, put someone else in the frame and disarmed the angry mob. Those who were fuming were still fuming, but then they were always going to be, unless he donated his services for the living wage. Everybody else smiled and got on with the washing-up. And when, this September, Lineker offered to take a cut on what was by then the BBC's highest salary – Evans having left – somehow that news leaked into the media. It was as beautifully played as the rest of Lineker's media career. He doesn't really need the BBC's money. He has so many other avenues – Walkers crisps, BT Sport, podcasts, TM Lewin shirts – he can afford to be the good guy. He might actually burnish his image, even open other revenue streams, by being the BBC man big enough to take a cut. Others have done it, too, but once again – he's Gary Lineker. This means more.

And, whatever the motivations of each individual act, a basic instinct towards the common good makes him different. Lineker is the son of Barry, a market trader, a greengrocer, a hard worker. Lots of early mornings, lots of standing out in all weathers. There are not many

2013
Signs up with NBC to work on its Premier League coverage. Participates in *Who Do You Think You Are?* and discovers that his great-great-great grandfather served time in Leicester Prison for poaching.

socialists pulling out market stalls. It is a life that tends to promote conservatism: the value of graft, the importance of earned wealth. And Barry produced a son who became one of the world's finest footballers. Again, a climate that fosters right-wing thinking. The sports team is the ultimate meritocracy, football in particular. There remain suspicions that cricket or rugby can be influenced by the right connections, the right teacher, the right school. Football is different. The working man's ballet, as Alan Hudson called it. Social background, social skills even, do not matter. A place in the team is the purest meritocracy, often involving huge personal sacrifice and relentless effort. The concept of the team may be socialist, but what it takes to get in are the values of pure conservatism. It is not just about the money, or low taxes. Footballers tack right because their career paths condition them that way.

So it is easy to imagine the political background from which Lineker originated. His middle name is Winston and probably not because his parents were huge fans of dancehall reggae. Lineker admitted that before Barry passed away – they had one of those awkward father-son relationships in which love was felt, but unspoken, until it was far too late – he could never bring himself to ask how his dad voted in the EU referendum, mainly because he was scared of the answer. Yet it is still there, in glimpses:

2014
Sets up his own production company called Goalhanger Films.

Lineker's political upbringing. Describing his schooldays, he recalls his loss of interest in history as a subject. "I used to enjoy it and then we had a teacher who seemed hell-bent on converting us to communism," he said. "I got Ungraded for history." Think about that, because we've all known teachers like that. They tend to be earnest Jeremy Corbyn types rather than Lenin in elbow patches. One imagines what passed for communist hectoring in the Lineker household would have been several Bolsheviks short of the full politburo. It is interesting, too, that Lineker's political persona has developed since he has left the single-minded meritocracy of the dressing-room behind. So this has been a journey. A more standard reaction to the criticism of his BBC salary from a person with Lineker's background would be a flick of the greying locks, and an echo of the entitled L'Oreal slogan: because I'm worth it.

Yet that is part of his balancing act. He may not be the voice of the people on Brexit, but he is not so distanced from what is said in pubs on most matters. The reason *A Hard Day's Night* works as a film, and *Give My Regards to Broad Street* doesn't, is because The Beatles felt like a gang you could be part of, while Paul and Linda McCartney and their celebrity friends were beyond ordinary imagination and experience. Lineker, on *Match of the Day*, contrives to make jokes with heroes of the English game, such as Alan

2014
Joins prime minister David Cameron at announcement of a school sport initiative.

2015
Remakes the first Walkers advert, called "Welcome home", to celebrate 20-year partnership. Is announced as the lead presenter of BT Sport's Champions League coverage. He and Danielle Bux divorce.

Shearer and Ian Wright, without ever giving the impression you would be excluded if bumping into them in the street. He presented *Match of the Day* in his boxers because, like all fans, he was pessimistic about his team's chances of success, and made a foolish promise around Leicester winning the league. Yet even standing half naked in front of the cameras he pulled it off: his body toned enough in middle age to be more triumph than humiliation, the act adding to his reputation as a good sport.

So Lineker is worth it. He holds *Match of the Day* together, dressed or undressed, effortlessly these days and, if anything, his social media persona adds to the profile of every programme, or event, he touches. On any given day, in between Brexit and random endorsements of a left-leaning, humanitarian nature, Lineker can be found plugging shows he is presenting, whether the resumption of the Champions League on BT Sport, or the running order of that night's *Match of the Day*. Come for Farage is a dick, stay for what time Manchester United are on; or vice versa. Stay for pithy observations on football, or cricket. Stay if you want to know the make of shirt he is wearing. It's whatever works, really; a superlative performance in the arena of modern media, skilfully judged and all his own doing.

And it is important that Lineker is the author, the

2016
Presents the first *Match of the Day* of the new season wearing only boxer shorts – after promising to do so if Leicester won the Premier League. Tweets that "treatment by some towards these young refugees is hideously racist and utterly heartless. What's happening to our country?" *The Sun* calls for him to be sacked from *Match of the Day*.

designer, of his own profile, because so many are not. In February 2018, a footballer for Manchester United, Jesse Lingard, received a tweet from an independent promotional group called I Love Manchester, an organisation that publicises life and events in the city. The message asked when Lingard and his team-mate Marcus Rashford were coming into the office for a few games of FIFA, the football computer game. Lingard replied: "Your not ready for me."

The problem subsequently was more than just grammatical. Lingard was, at the time, attending a memorial service at Old Trafford for the victims of the Munich air disaster. Condemnation was fierce and immediate. And then a hasty follow-up message appeared. "A member of my media team inadvertently replied to a tweet this afternoon on my Twitter profile during the Munich memorial service at Old Trafford. I was unaware as I was attending the service at the time, and don't condone the post or the timing in anyway," Lingard wrote.

Or maybe he didn't, this being confirmation that Lingard's social media profile, his banter, his personality, was quite often the work of a faceless media professional acting on instinct. Worse, the person Lingard employed to fulfil this function was either semi-literate or thought his boss was, so dropped in bad English deliberately, to make

2018
Suffers with Rio Ferdinand and Alan Shearer while presenting England's World Cup semi-final defeat to Croatia.

the tweets more convincing. In this climate of deception, it is significant that Lineker's thoughts are authentic, his views or his mis-steps his own. This is not managed. Like it or not, this is him, unplugged.

So when, in May, Lineker's podcast partner Danny Baker became a figure of public opprobrium, all eyes turned to Lineker for his reaction. Baker marked the birth of Archie, son of the Duke and Duchess of Sussex, with a photograph of two toffs beside a small chimpanzee wearing a bowler hat, suit, overcoat and carrying a cane. "Royal baby arrives," read the caption. Baker was making his usual joke about privilege, but the Duchess's family is black. So it was seen as an intentional racist insult, mainly by those who have no clue about Baker, either professionally or personally. The BBC sacked him immediately, of course; yet still we waited for Lineker's reaction. He said, nothing. No condemnation, but no message of support either. Others, familiar with Baker's work, came to his defence, insisting he had intended no connection between Duchess and simian, other than to make a humorous point about wealth and class. Animals in human garb were a regular trope on his shows. The mitigations were all there. Yet from Lineker, still nothing.

And then, when the storm had subsided, and Baker was beginning to work again, and there was less heat and

2018
Announces his support for People's Vote, calling for a public vote on the final Brexit deal between the UK and the EU.

Becomes BBC's highest-paid on-air talent, earning £1.75m a year. Is only big-name male star not to take a pay cut.

more understanding, and slightly more than six weeks had elapsed, it was leaked, through an "insider", that Baker and Lineker would work together again. "Gary has decided to stand by his pal," an unnamed source told the tabloids. And he did, sort of. But he was also mindful to test the water first. And by the time Lineker finally spoke about Baker it was September. The chimp tweet was sent in May. The reason Lineker controls his own output is that, at 58, he knows as much about media management, crisis management, and the point on the Venn diagram where they meet as any adviser. When he recently received an overture from a rival broadcaster, he was confident enough to entertain the emissary at home, without the presence of agents or strategists. Even those born into the world of entertainment are rarely that bold.

Inescapably, this is a man ageing well, a man confident enough to engage enthusiastically with celebrity and popularity wars that have destroyed lesser intellects. Lineker recalls that at his first school, Caldecote Juniors, he was caned for being cheeky, but it is precisely this attribute that wins him so many admirers now. That, and a perceived enlightenment. Beyond having a good Brexit, Lineker is having an outstanding second act in life. "It's been a bit like my football," he has said of his various inspired choices. "I've made my runs into space at the right time." ◖.

2019
Volunteers to take a pay cut from BBC. *Behind Closed Doors*, his book co-written with Danny Baker, is published.

They say you shouldn't meet your heroes. *Zelda Perkins* not only met hers, she produced the musical he staged in his dying days

The final bow

"I know nothing about producing theatre," I said. I was talking to the theatre impresario and film producer, Robert Fox. And I needed a job. He had suggested that I might become his associate producer.

I didn't feel that the theatre studies module of my degree many moons before would qualify me but, it turned out, my years working for (the now disgraced) Harvey Weinstein and Miramax, not to mention my enthusiasm for the plays of David Hare, did the trick.

And the first project I was given to manage was Hare's *Skylight* at the Wyndham's Theatre in the West End, starring Bill Nighy and Carey Mulligan. Producing it, Robert had predicted, would be a much easier and more joyful experience than producing a film. And so began a very happy partnership that continues to this day.

When I joined him, Robert was engrossed in a big Andrew Lloyd Webber musical called *Stephen Ward*. He needed someone to take some of the load of the plethora of exciting projects he had on his slate. These ranged, he told me, from a new Martin McDonagh play, something with Nile Rodgers of Chic, another with Hugh Jackman, a new television series about the Royal Family by Peter Morgan, a film script and, oh, potentially a musical with David Bowie.

Wait. David Bowie? He paused. It's in development, he said, but before that we need to cast someone to play the Queen in the London revival of *The Audience* as Helen Mirren was moving to play Her Majesty on Broadway.

But I was still stuck on Bowie.

The world of theatre production was to be a happy discovery for me. After my bruising experience with Weinstein (that's another story) it was a revelation to work in an industry where the writer, director, set designer and other creatives were treated as artists. Producers in theatre respected all their work and did not try to change endings to suit test audiences or tell a director how to do his or her job.

There must be at least five different types of film producer plus more production managers and associates and executives. They wield budgets of millions and crews of hundreds. In a theatre, the producer has a smaller crew and a finite run on the stage but is directly responsible for all aspects of a production, from budget to casting to renting the theatre space. I loved it.

In 2013 I began to get involved with the Bowie project. It was made clear that I would be unlikely to have direct contact with David himself. I was both thrilled and secretly relieved. For me, as for many people, he was an awe-inspiring figure, one of the great artists of our time and provider of the soundtrack to my life.

Working in the film industry had introduced me to many of my idols and, almost without exception, I'd been

New York was home to David Bowie for more than 20 years and where he recorded his final album, 'Blackstar', and staged his musical, 'Lazarus'. He once said that America 'filled a vast expanse of my imagination' disappointed every time. The thought that David Bowie might be the same was too much to bear. Supposing he had halitosis? Or was a mean-spirited egotist? Or frankly just an ordinary human? I was more than content not to meet him.

It turned out that in 2005 David had given Robert a copy of the Walter Tevis novel, *The Man Who Fell to Earth*. This was the book on which Nicolas Roeg had based his 1976 film of the same name, starring Bowie. His appearance in the film had become an enormously important part of the Bowie iconography and reinforced his "alien" reputation. Images from the film adorned the covers of his albums *Station to Station* (1976) and *Low* (1977), not to mention countless magazine covers and posters. There was no explanation for this precious gift, just an inscription in the flyleaf:

> *Robert,*
>
> *'Im not a human being at all' (Thomas Jerome Newton)*
>
> *(SSSHHH!! David Bowie)*
>
> *David*
> *2005*

Now, eight years later, David told Robert he wanted to make a musical called *Lazarus* about the character (Thomas Jerome Newton) he had played in the film – an alien trapped on Earth. Robert had then introduced David to Enda Walsh, a hugely talented Irish writer, and work began on the outline of the show. Suddenly, in 2014, the project was fast-tracked at David's behest.

I thought no more – then – of this sudden acceleration; such things are common in the creative industry.

We arranged for David to meet Ivo van Hove, the avant garde Belgian director whose production of Arthur Miller's *A View from the Bridge* had wildly impressed London critics and audiences. It had especially hit a note with Robert when thinking of a pairing for the Bowie project, and once David's collaborator Henry Hey was added as musical director, the team was complete.

We set up a workshop in New York, where Bowie lived, to see how the material and music we had at this point worked with actors. This was not as easy as usual to arrange because we had been told not to give any details about the project to agents: no script, no music, no clue as to who had originated the project. The only thing we could say was that "a world-famous composer/performer" was involved. This made it extremely difficult to attract the sort of cast we wanted but all our instructions from the Bowie camp were to keep the utmost secrecy at all times.

I was allowed contact with David's business manager, Bill Zysblat, in New York but still only Robert could communicate directly with David, or Coco Schwab – the woman who had been at his side since the early 70s and who was known to guard him fiercely. Coco and David often seemed to have one voice. Robert's creative questions to David were often answered by Coco in the plural: "we think", "we would like".

Gradually, and despite the mystery, we assembled a cast to workshop the material and see what we had. Each actor was asked to sign a non-disclosure agreement before being given sight of the rough script and song-list for the day.

In December 2014 we all gathered in a large rehearsal space on 42nd Street. The room was electric with anticipation: Henry Hey at the piano, a circle of chairs for the actors, and a small group of those of us involved thus far, watching and waiting for a legend to appear among us. Beside the piano was a chair for Ivo and a small camera on a large tripod. Introductions were made but there was still no sign of Bowie.

Only when the time came for the actors to begin did the message come: David was ill (flu, we were told) but he would be watching from home on that camera. It blinked green when he was viewing, we learnt, so no one could take their eyes off it. Henry had an earpiece through which he was communicating with David but otherwise there was no tangible sign of his presence apart from that camera. It was a fittingly surreal start to a production that eventually grew, according to the *Rolling Stone* critic, into "a surrealistic tour de force".

What only four people in that room knew (and I wasn't one of them) was that David's "flu" was, in fact, cancer.

When the production came to rehearsals, David attended as often as possible in person. He wanted the show to be produced close to him, so the off-Broadway New York Theatre Workshop (noted for its productions of new and challenging works) was the natural choice to co-produce the project. They had close ties with the writer and director

David Bowie
with 'Lazarus'
director Ivo van
Hove during
rehearsals,
which took
place at the
New York

Theatre
Workshop.
The venue was
chosen as it
was so close
to Bowie's
home in the
East Village

and the theatre was in walking distance from Bowie's East Village home.

Reports from Ivo and the cast all told of David's enthusiasm and creative generosity. He put everyone at ease as they sang his iconic songs to him. David wanted each cast member to own the songs, to interpret them as they wished, to live them in their experience. This generosity and collaborative nature had shown itself early in the process when David had asked Enda to choose the songs he wanted for the show. Enda did not make the obvious choices and David, with the help of Henry, then carefully rearranged the 13 songs for the stage. He also wrote four new songs specifically for the production, one of them being the title track *Lazarus*, which would become his first US top-40 single since the 1980s, streamed by nearly 9 million people in the week of its release.

Marketing a musical show without being able to give any information about what it would be about or what music it would contain was a challenge. We had strict instructions from David that we should not give an outline of the story or music to the press. All we could say was that it took its inspiration from *The Man Who Fell to Earth*. He wanted people to come to *Lazarus* without preconceptions. David made it clear to us that he did not want the production or the narrative to be explained: as with the cast taking ownership of his songs, he wanted people to have their own individual experience of what they saw on stage and how it made them feel, no matter how confused they may be.

People at the New York Theatre Workshop were nervous about this strategy and I didn't blame them. Even the artwork for the production was mysterious:

a moody evening East Village skyline. David had been presented with several other ideas: Major Tom-style space helmets, rockets in huge TV screens – all images that related to Bowie and to the content of the show. But he emphatically chose the most obscure image that revealed almost nothing.

He would make no statement for the press, declined every request for an interview and would do no publicity but when tickets went on sale in early October they sold out in hours. Theatre doesn't work like rock'n'roll; it is virtually unheard of for an entire run to sell out hours after going on sale. Resale sites were soon asking $1,000 a ticket.

It didn't hurt that our Newton was Michael C Hall, a star in his own right having won a Golden Globe for his performance in the television series, *Dexter*. And the show would run for only a few weeks. But there was no doubt whose name was selling the tickets.

As the dress rehearsal approached Robert was suddenly taken gravely ill, so I had to go to New York without him. Arriving late in a taxi straight from the airport, I was frazzled and had a headache, my nerves only slightly calmed by Coco informing me that she and David would not be there.

After brief hellos with our co-producers from the New York Theatre Workshop, I took my seat in the centre of the auditorium and made sure there was no one to my left or right. I wanted to watch undisturbed by the technical staff or the few invited guests. I had notes to write. I would not only have to relay my opinion to Robert later that night but immediately after the show, in Robert's place, give my thoughts and suggestions on the production to the director, designer, sound, light and music heads of department. No one there knew this was my first foray into musical theatre.

The lights went down and a story I thought I knew well began. What unfolded on stage, however, was unlike anything I had ever seen. It was raw, challenging, heartbreaking, confusing and deeply uncomfortable to watch. I sat mesmerised, feelings of euphoria and horror fighting for supremacy. This was a graphic, surreal and highly stylised production that tore furiously at the depths of loneliness and lost hope in a wild journey, peopled with characters whose existence in reality or fantasy were difficult to distinguish.

It was hard to describe, featuring as it did balloon-popping, milk-sliding, serial killing, copious amounts of gin and blood, with replays of the live action appearing on a giant television screen. All this might be enough to discombobulate the regular theatre-goer and David's songs coming to life in new ways might confuse those expecting something more familiar. All this, I later discovered, was to Bowie's absolute design and delight.

When at last the lights came up, I rushed to the loo to get my mind straight and ready to talk to Ivo and the director of the New York Theatre Workshop. What could I say to everyone that would be honest, coherent but still encouraging?

As I returned to the foyer a small, grey-haired woman

From left: actors Michael C Hall, Michael Esper and Cristin Milioti, and director Ivo van Hove, outside the New York Theatre Workshop in November 2015. Casting and early rehearsals took place amid great secrecy. All the actors knew was that a 'world-famous composer/performer' was involved grabbed my arm. It was the elusive Coco. "You must speak to David," she said, propelling me back into the auditorium. She and David had been there to watch the show after all. My heart fell to the floor.

I was pushed towards him, protesting to Coco as I went that David should speak to Ivo and the other creatives first. But David clambered over the two rows of seats separating us, pulled me into the aisle and enveloped me in an enormous hug. "Zelda," he said. "We meet at last!"

He was wearing a baseball cap and an overcoat, though the room was warm, but there was no disguising his pallor and that he was struggling for breath. However, his eyes were ablaze and he immediately started talking excitedly about what we had just witnessed. He wanted to know exactly what I thought. Did I like the new arrangements of his songs? What did I think of the choreography? Wasn't it marvellously tangled and surprising? He was holding my hands (or was I holding his?) and I found I couldn't break his gaze, or not be infected by his delight. My inner voice of doubt and commercial worry was immediately silenced. I had been reminded that the true artist does not fear the viewer's gaze.

David Bowie was officially the most delicious smelling man on Earth. I know this because of that hug. I didn't shower that night and slept, smiling, with the intense, clean smell of him in my hair and on my pillow. Nothing about him had disappointed after all. But less than two months later he was gone for ever.

It was not until I saw him myself at that dress rehearsal that I saw the truth of the situation. He was ill. Terminally ill, as it turned out. Those around me seemed not to have seen it, or had chosen not to acknowledge it. Perhaps that was easily done. Perhaps that enormous enthusiasm, which seemed to light David from within, blinded those working with him to his gaunt appearance and laboured breathing. I find I can easily believe that.

And his workrate was astonishing. He may have been ill and coping with the treatment but he was not only helping create *Lazarus*, he was also working on his final album, the majestic *Blackstar*. In fact, the lead song for the theatre project became the second single and video released for *Blackstar*, poignantly – or perhaps purposefully – on David's birthday, 8 January. Two days later his death was announced.

While we had been in New York attending the start of rehearsals in 2015, he had been on set filming the *Lazarus* video. Strapped to a vertical hospital bed, made up as a dying man, his voice thin and breathy, he sang: "Look up here I'm in heaven, I've got scars that can't be seen... I'm in danger, I've got nothing left to lose."

How was it that none of us heard what he was so clearly saying?

The *Blackstar* and *Lazarus* videos and lyrics now seem so obviously stuffed with clues. Did no one hear or see these clues that were screaming through the songs and dialogue about the frailty of mortality – his own mortality?

The opening night for *Lazarus* was on 7 December 2015. David attended. The Thin White Duke made flesh took the curtain call with the cast to the surprise and delight of the audience. He took a last and extravagant bow on stage, laughing with unbridled joy and holding hands with the cast and the director of the musical he had for so long hoped to realise. It was his last public appearance.

On the morning his death was announced, the cast were scheduled to record the cast album of the show. Shell-shocked, they gathered in a recording studio and sang their grief out for Bowie – each song carrying a new resonance.

Critics reappraised their initial reviews of the show, which suddenly became more cohesive and coherent to them. A shrine of candles, flowers and pictures soon covered the pavement outside the theatre. The outpouring of grief from all around the world was a tidal wave, fuelled no doubt by the quiet dignity and purpose with which David had left.

To many it seemed almost stage-managed. David didn't want explanations and it is not for me to try to explain his art but *Lazarus* and *Blackstar* now seem clearly works about his impending death. And as we keep discovering, a trail of clues and surprises was laid along the way. One of these, which makes my eyes prick even now, was the album cover of *Blackstar*. A month after the vinyl version of the album went on sale, it was discovered that if the sleeve was exposed to direct sunlight the black star graphic on the cover dispersed to reveal a galaxy of stars – a sweet and happy gift from beyond the grave. Jonathan Barnbrook, who designed Bowie's album covers, including the cast album artwork and the *Lazarus* theatre programme, has since admitted that there are several hidden "easter eggs" still to be found.

But *Lazarus* did not end here for me. We brought

the production to London but were not content that it should sit in a West End playhouse. It needed a venue that gave the audience the full experience of the seven-piece rock'n'roll band who were on stage throughout. Their sound had been so carefully curated by David and Henry to be as intense as any live rock concert it had to be heard in the right acoustic environment. In the end we built a huge and dramatic space, seating a thousand, near King's Cross and the show gained the scale and volume that David wanted.

Each night the atmosphere in the bar before the show had the energy of a concert, or a one-off event. And each night the show reports detailed the visceral effect the production had on the audience. Tears, anger, outpourings of love and emotion on a scale astonishing to the staff. The critics, however, were divided.

As for me, I believe *Lazarus* is ahead of its time and will only continue to give more and more as time passes. More secrets revealed themselves each time I saw it and even after more than 20 viewings it had an overwhelming effect on me. Tears came always but I could never predict at which point. Laughter, too, and I left always a little wiser.

Bowie once said: "I'd like my death to be as interesting as my life has been." Oh, how he succeeded. ◠●

The final bow: David Bowie poses for his long-time photographer Jimmy King in what is believed to be his last official photoshoot. The image was posted on his website and Instagram account on 8 January 2016, his 69th birthday and the day his final album 'Blackstar' was released. He died two days later

Murder by

In 2017, two United Nations investigators were
murdered in Congo, their killers filming the
cold-blooded atrocity. Nearly three years later,
no one has been convicted for it. *Tristan McConnell*
reports on the shameful failures of the
Congolese authorities and the UN itself

translation

MURDER

In the video of their deaths, Zaida Catalán and Michael J Sharp are shepherded, shoeless, through scrubby forest. The two United Nations investigators, whose job it was to recommend human rights abusers and arms embargo busters for sanctions, were killed on a Sunday afternoon in March 2017 in Kasai, a southern region of the Democratic Republic of Congo that is larger than the United Kingdom but with barely a stretch of unpotholed paved road.

They are accompanied by at least 13 men: some wear red bandanas, some carry 12-gauge shotguns, others hold knives. Sharp talks in French; Catalán is silent. The two are ordered to sit on the ground facing each other. A few moments later, Sharp is shot at close range, then Catalán. She stumbles to her feet and runs a few paces before falling. Then two men take turns using a knife to cut off Catalán's head. The film, which surfaced two weeks after the killings, abruptly ends.

Catalán, 36, a Swede, and Sharp, 34, an American, were members of the Group of Experts, a UN Security Council-mandated team of six investigators monitoring war crimes in Congo. Catalán's expertise was in humanitarian issues, while Sharp, the group's leader, specialised in armed groups.

Two and a half years later the killings remain unsolved, but slowly the layers of deliberate deceptions, false accounts, face-saving cover-ups and callous disregard – both in Congo and at the UN – have begun to dissolve, the tale of a deadly ambush by murderous rebels giving way to something closer to the truth, and far darker.

UN troops in Kasai. Previous page:
   Catalán and Sharp (left) and
   scenes from the fatal video

LIES

The site of the Catalán and Sharp murders was only 45
miles from Kananga, the provincial capital where they had
last been seen on the morning of 12 March 2017. But in
Kasai that counts as remote. It took more than two weeks
for Catalán and Sharp's colleagues to find them. They were
carelessly buried, soil heaped hurriedly into shallow graves,
the heel of a foot left poking through the earth in the forest
clearing where they were shot dead.

A forensic team in white hazmat suits disinterred the
bodies close to the village of Moyo Musuila. Although
there was little doubt they were indeed those of Catalán
and Sharp, identification was hampered by the absence
of Catalán's head. An autopsy later found that she had

Zaida Catalán and Michael Sharp
are the first UN investigators to be
murdered while doing their jobs

bled to death after being shot multiple times, and was subsequently decapitated. Sharp was also killed by multiple gunshots, including to the head. The recovery of pellets from wounds in both bodies suggested the murder weapon in each case was a shotgun.

Catalán and Sharp are the first – and so far only – UN investigators to be killed in the line of duty anywhere in the world, and Kinshasa was eager that blame should fall on a Kasai-based insurgency known as Kamwina Nsapu that was challenging central authority and irritating the president.

Six weeks after their deaths, officials in Kinshasa held a press conference, where they revealed the existence of the 6min 17sec video, shot on a mobile phone, of the killings. "The images speak for themselves," the then information minister Lambert Mende said after playing it for the journalists. "It is not our soldiers that we see in the video executing the two UN workers but the terrorists of the

Kamwina Nsapu militia." The government also took the opportunity to air another snuff movie, this time showing headless bodies in police uniforms, to bolster the claim that decapitation is a signature of the militia.

After the video's release, the government moved quickly to prosecute some of those who appear in the video and a prize witness named Jean Bosco Mukanda quickly came forward claiming to have seen the murders, providing testimony implicating local Kamwina Nsapu leaders. By June a military tribunal in Kananga had taken up the case. The government's simple story, which it laid out at the trial with Mukanda's ready testimony, was that Catalán and Sharp naively wandered into a conflict, were waylaid by Kamwina Nsapu bandits, robbed and killed. This hermetic narrative was neat, convenient and suspicious.

POLITICS

President Joseph Kabila's corrupt, violent regime had kept successive Groups of Experts busy since he succeeded his assassinated father in 2001, presiding over the looting of the country and continued conflict. Despite stepping down in December – reluctantly and two years late – he remains powerful, the puppet master to his co-opted successor Félix Tshisikedi. Parliament and the judiciary are still stacked with his allies and loyalists and it is Kabila's, not Tshisikedi's, presidential portrait that still hangs on walls around the country.

Violence in Congo most often afflicts the eastern Kivus and Ituri provinces – where an Ebola outbreak is currently spreading – but the Kasai region where Catalán and

Sharp were killed has its own history of political turmoil. Independent Congo's first crisis began there and successive presidents found the region to be a thorn in their sides. Congo's most tenacious opposition politician, Étienne Tshisekedi (father of Félix), was born in Kananga and made Kasai his stronghold as he opposed first Mobutu, then his successor, Laurent Kabila (father of Joseph), and finally Joseph Kabila. In retaliation, Kasai has suffered even more abject neglect than the rest of the country, leaving its residents deeply impoverished.

As the date for the 2016 elections loomed and Kabila sought avenues to stay in power, an attempt was made to co-opt an influential traditional leader in Kasai for political gain. But the move went awry and the chief, known as Kamwina Nsapu, was killed, triggering the insurgency that bears his name. Violent confrontations saw soldiers armed with assault rifles and heavy weapons battle villagers carrying shotguns and knives. Even by Congolese standards the scale of violence was "alarming and unusual", said Ida Sawyer of Human Rights Watch.

Scores of mass graves were filled with the remains of Kamwina Nsapu fighters, or civilians suspected of supporting them, and villages were burned. Around 5,000 people were killed and, at the height of the upheaval, a million and a half people were forced from their homes.

Jason Stearns, at New York University's Congo Research Group and one of Sharp's predecessors as coordinator of the Group of Experts, told me that the Congolese army's extreme brutality in Kasai was "unprecedented" even by the standards of a military well-known for its excesses. "You have this local, ragtag militia group that protested against the Congolese government and in response the army goes in and responds with extraordinary and often indiscriminate violence. This was obviously very organised: there were orders given to deal with this in the way they dealt with it."

Having failed dismally to win Kasai over, the unrest there became one of the various reasons the Kabila government offered for delaying elections. The vote never happened and, by early 2017, the president was under increasing pressure both at home and abroad after ignoring constitutional term limits, refusing to cede power and violently suppressing the countrywide protests that followed.

Then, a mobile phone video showing soldiers executing civilians was leaked to the press, leading the UN's human rights chief to call for an inquiry. These atrocities were exactly the kind of thing the Group of Experts was appointed to investigate and so Catalán and Sharp set off from Kananga into the febrile heart of Congo's latest conflagration. Their murders were instantly inseparable from Congo's fraught political context and a history of impunity that begins at the top.

EVIDENCE

The government's version of Catalán and Sharp's murders is beguilingly simple, playing to stereotypical notions of chaotic, innate brutality and outsider naivety, but is contradicted by a close viewing of the very evidence on which it rests, the mobile phone video.

Just before the killings begin, an obscuring cover is removed from the lens, dramatically improving the

The Congolese army is accused of
'unprecedented' brutality in Kasai

image clarity for the crucial scenes to follow. Catalán
and Sharp walk barefoot, having already been stripped
of their possessions. At the moment the shooting starts
at least one man darts away in surprise while others
appear prepped and act efficiently. "One thing that's clear
from the video is that this was an organised hit," said
Stearns. "This was not some guys at a roadblock who all
of a sudden got upset."

The video's audio track, too, contains evidence.
Kamwina Nsapu is a local movement and its members
speak a local language called Tshiluba yet in the video, two
men off-camera speak French and Lingala – a language
commonly spoken in the capital and among the security
forces – and bark orders in broken Tshiluba, sometimes
sounding as if they are talking on a phone. "That's a big

deal," Stearns said. "It would be strange for outsiders to be involved in this militia."

As investigators, Catalán and Sharp kept meticulous records, including an audio recording of a meeting with a Kamwina Nsapu elder in a Kananga hotel the day before their murders. Transcripts produced independently by the UN and French broadcaster Radio France Internationale (RFI) show that a crucial exchange was mistranslated: the elder warns the investigators against travel to a town called Bunkonde, since he cannot ensure their safety there. Instead, Catalán and Sharp are told: "You can arrive in Bunkonde, there is nothing... You will pass without problems."

Their translator, Thomas Nkashama, fixer José Tshibuabua and guide Betu Tshintela collude in the deceit. The next morning Catalán and Sharp headed for Bunkonde, and their deaths.

According to a former colleague, Catalán and Sharp's main focus in Kasai was not in fact army atrocities and mass graves, but Kamwina Nsapu's practice of recruiting children and drugging them for battle. However, the attention on mass graves in the weeks before their visit meant there was "a misperception" about their presence in Kasai, one that may have proven deadly.

Subsequent investigations by some UN officials, RFI and others have revealed that those responsible for misleading Catalán and Sharp during the hotel meeting had all worked for Congolese intelligence and security services. "All the people who lied to the experts during that recorded interview were linked in some way with the intelligence service," RFI's Sonia Rolley told me.

Documents show that Tshibuabua was a member of the

Agence Nationale de Renseignements (ANR), Congo's national intelligence agency, and a cousin of Tshintela, who had also worked for the agency, while Nkashama was a member of the country's pervasive immigration-cum-security service, the Direction Générale de Migration (DGM). All three were in touch with local army commander Colonel Jean de Dieu Mambweni.

The meeting was a set-up. "It appears they were deliberately tricked," Sawyer said. "All of the research we have conducted indicates government involvement, a plot planned by the intelligence services to portray Kamwina Nsapu as terrorists," and to shift the narrative of atrocities from the army to the militia.

FAILINGS

At UN headquarters in New York, the first response to the murders of its own people was bureaucratic: a board of inquiry was set up in the weeks after Catalán and Sharp's bodies were found and narrowly mandated to discover whether proper UN safety procedures had been followed.

The confidential 47-page report was handed over to the Security Council in August 2017. Its account of the killings tracked closely with the Congolese government's, ignoring the available evidence of state involvement. It found that "the violent acts of a group of Congolese perpetrators, likely militia members from the Kasai province, were responsible for the deaths" of Catalán and Sharp. It mentioned that one of the experts was carrying "relatively large amounts of cash" and suggested that robbery was the motive and blithely concluded that "information circulating regarding the possible involvement of various government individuals or organisations" was insufficient to apportion blame.

Late last year the Swedish broadcaster Sveriges Television revealed an audio recording of the board of inquiry's head, Greg Starr, telling Catalán and Sharp's bereaved families that despite the evidence provided by others in the UN, as well as RFI, he did not implicate Congolese officials in his report because there is "a line that I don't want to cross" in order to keep the investigation going, however inadequate or compromised it was.

"The board of inquiry had access to the recording, to our translation and linguistic analysis of the video, but all the information that we used in our investigation is barely mentioned, or quickly dismissed," said Rolley of RFI.

Catalán and Sharp's former UN colleague told me: "I've worked through the report from beginning to end and to me they haven't looked at the translations that they've been receiving of what was talked about on the video, or at the meeting the day before." Instead, the colleague added, the board of inquiry relied on a government-provided translator for the recordings. "For some reason they didn't want to deal with this."

When the UN made a summary of the report public it was met with dismay. "The board of inquiry bottom line was that Michael and Zaida were partly guilty for their own deaths and the UN did the best job it possibly could in the field and at headquarters," Stearns said. "This interpretation of the available facts is very sympathetic toward the government but not toward the victims."

The criticism of the board's work – including from

family members of the deceased – led the UN to send a second team to Congo in late 2017, led by Canadian lawyer Robert Petit, a former prosecutor of the Khmer Rouge, tasked to "support" the Congolese prosecution – code for trying to ensure it would not be a sham.

Petit faced obstruction. In a confidential note to the Security Council in April last year, Petit wrote that his team was being stymied and concluded: "It is quite clear that the security apparatus in Kinshasa continues to interfere with the judicial process and controls access to key witnesses and suspects."

Petit's is not the first investigation to be hindered by Congolese authorities. The Federal Bureau of Investigation and Swedish prosecutors were also obstructed by a lack of co-operation: the Swedes wrote in a frustrated statement in November 2017, just as Petit was getting to work, of the "major difficulties with regard to being completely dependent on evidence in Congo and co-operation with Congo is not working". They could not "rule out that people closely related to the regime in Congo were involved in the murder" of Catalán and Sharp.

TRIAL

The trial at the military court in Kananga began three months after the murders but with only two of the 17 suspects in custody. The men who had misled Catalán and Sharp in the hotel meeting, and been among the last to see them alive, were neither suspects nor witnesses. Hearings were held in fits and starts, with lengthy adjournments and little discernible progress.

Police arrest a man protesting at
further election delays in 2018

The rush to trial led UN police, in a confidential briefing
note, to bemoan the "lack of rigor and professionalism"
displayed by the prosecution while a confidential UN
summary of investigations sent to diplomats in Kinshasa
raised concerns about the trustworthiness of the
prosecution's main witness, Mukanda, who it described as
"an active collaborator" with the army, and a man who had
been repeatedly introduced to some UN staff by Congolese
army officers during the search for Catalán and Sharp.

But gradually something approaching the truth is
coming into focus. In late 2017, during a ten-month
adjournment, Tshibuabua and Nkashama – the fixer and
translator at the hotel meeting – were taken into custody
by Congolese security services (whether to put them on
trial or protect them from questioning was unclear as Petit
was denied access to them.) Months later the one-time

star prosecution witness, Mukanda, was himself arrested after prosecutors scrutinised his phone records, then, in December, Colonel Mambweni was also taken into custody on suspicion of organising the murders. All four have been charged with involvement in the killings.

The trial resumed in mid-September before a higher military court, also in Kasai. There are now 47 suspects, though only 23 are in detention. The others were either never arrested or among a group of five who escaped from prison in May, including the only person to have admitted appearing in the murder video.

But crucially, Mambweni, Mukanda, Nkashama and Tshibuabua are all in the dock, the very men who, for their intelligence and military connections, suspicious behaviour and telephone links, fell under suspicion in confidential internal UN documents just weeks after the murders, long before the first trial hearings and long before the UN's own deeply flawed inquiry.

TRUTH

Catalán's final call, made half an hour before her death, was to her younger sister, Elizabeth Morseby, at home in Kalmar, Sweden. Catalán did not speak. "I could hear lots of male voices talking and then Zaida breathing in the background," Morseby told me. "My mother was standing next to me and she was worried immediately." The call lasted a little more than a minute then cut off.

Bereaved, confused and faced with conflicting information, the families of Catalán and Sharp have been confronted by the very thing the investigators had sought to end. "Zaida wanted to end impunity for perpetrators and that is what we want too, justice not only for Michael and Zaida but for all the people in those graves," Morseby said. "The ones who killed Michael and Zaida are responsible for that mess over there, murdering their own people. I want them prosecuted, I want them in jail."

Even if the colonel and his alleged accomplices are found guilty, who gave the orders? Who else was involved? "We want them to dig deeper," she said. The families have learned to expect little of the Congolese judiciary and have been dismayed to find the UN credulous of a false narrative and then constrained in their later investigations under Petit.

The failure to find the truth of the murders is tantamount to declaring open season on dozens of UN expert groups, panels and sanctions monitors, all of which work within the sphere of influence of regimes potentially hostile to them.

"It is crucial to get to the bottom of what happened and ensure that the real perpetrators and commanders are held to account," said Sawyer. "If we don't, it sends the message that those responsible for such a heinous crime can get away with it, and that sets a dangerous precedent in Congo and across the world."

Truth and justice would comfort the families, too. "Let's have some accountability; let's find out who did this, who ordered this," Michael's father, John Sharp, told me. But, showing remarkable forbearance, he urged a pursuit of restorative rather than simply punitive justice. "Let's see if we can find some kind of redemptive solution that will go towards creating less suffering for the people of Congo," he said. "More violence isn't the answer." ᴓ●

BY | KEITH BLACKMORE

Flying on instruments

PAGE 86

LANCASTER • BOMBER COMMAND

Sqd Ldr Donald McKenzie Blackmore DFC

21/10/1919 — 8/1/1998

Donald Blackmore never wanted
to talk about it but his son, Keith,
needed to know what his late father,
an RAF pilot, did in the war...

MY FATHER WOULD HAVE BEEN A HUNDRED THIS OCTOBER. When he died, 21 years ago now, I was working at *The Times*. A considerate colleague from the obits department asked me kindly if I thought my father deserved an obituary. I declined. Don't ask me why. Embarrassment? Confusion? Diffidence? Distress? I have no satisfactory answer.

I've cursed myself ever since – not just because as the years have passed plenty of lesser lives have been celebrated in those pages; or because it would have made him proud, had he somehow been aware of it; nor because our grieving family would have taken some comfort in it. No, because he deserved the small honour that a place in The Thunderer's pages accords, and was denied it by his son's foolish modesty on his behalf.

++++++

So here is how that obituary might have begun: Donald McKenzie Blackmore was born in London on 21 October 1919 but raised in Bath, and a Somerset drawl would occasionally surface at moments of excitement and almost always when, in later years, he returned to the West Country.

His father, Alfred, was a stage manager in London's West End and his mother, Edith, an actress. Alfred abandoned Edith when Donald was tiny, leaving her to cope with two children and no certain means of earning a living.

She then took what must have been a hard decision for her but an even harder one for Donald, then aged five. She sent him by boat to Canada to live with distant relations of his estranged father. His younger brother remained in Bath, with her. Donald did not come home, or see his mother and brother again, for seven years.

By then, she had married a cousin, Benjamin, who was a master butcher for the Co-Op in Bath. At 14, Donald reluctantly left the school he had only barely joined to work for Benjamin and learn the butcher's trade. The reconstructed family needed the money. But as soon as he could, at the end of 1937 or early 1938 and against some family resistance, Donald joined the Royal Air Force.

His stepfather, no doubt influenced by the gassing of his own brother during the Great War and perhaps also anxious not to lose a valued young assistant, was dismayed. Still, it must have been apparent that his stepson's unusual facility with numbers was wasted at the butcher's counter.

So Donald's life was transformed.

»»»»»»

Here, a word about my sources. The primary source is, of course, 21 years gone and another, my mother, Frances, met my father after the war. And that primary source, typically of his generation, was extremely reluctant to talk about the war and the part he played in it. Even the version of his early life, outlined above, came from him only when I had children of my own. So I have just his word for it and my memory of what he told me.

When I was going through his affairs after his death I found that he had been making regular donations – and perhaps doing so all his life – to Dr Barnardo's (as it was then), the charity for homeless and orphaned children. He'd never mentioned that once to me.

On those rare occasions when he did pronounce on the subject of the war, his language would be sprinkled with the slang of his RAF years: "old boy", "flap", "gubbins" and "prang", for example, and "flying on instruments" (for pressing on while not being able to see where you are going). Old friends sometimes called him Crash, apparently because he didn't.

All this was tantalising for a small boy, anxious to have his theories of his father's heroism confirmed – and infuriating for this old boy, who expects something less but can't help hoping for something more.

I recall him saying that he started as an armourer, but since no such rank then existed in the RAF I surmise that, imperfectly educated as he was, he must have begun as an Aircraftman No 2 – an "Erk" as the lower ranks were called at the time. Potential must have been recognised because, by the time the RAF's bombing campaign reached its height in 1943-44, he had been back to Canada to learn to fly and become a Pilot Officer, flying Avro Lancasters deep into Germany.

By the end of the war he was a Flight Lieutenant. By the time he left the RAF, just after I was born in 1957, he was a Squadron Leader.

My mother remembers that he left because, at nearly 40, his reflexes were no longer fast enough to fly jets – although it's also possible that he had simply completed the 20 years he had originally signed up to serve.

In any case, he headed into retirement from the RAF entitled to append to his name the initials DFC, having been awarded the Distinguished Flying Cross – crudely put, the third highest award for valour available to airmen after the Victoria Cross and the Distinguished Service Order.

He naturally refused to discuss this, too, only heightening his son's fevered speculations. The family rumour, possibly invented by one of my aunts, was that he had been the inspiration for Nevil Shute's wartime novel, *Pastoral*, a love story set amid the tensions of a bomber pilot approaching the final operations of his tour.

It had some of the heroism I was looking for but its protagonist, one Peter Marshall, would have been at least five years older than my father. More crushing still, it was written in 1944. The author, a pilot himself, would have had to go some to have captured any of my father's exploits, whatever they might have been.

And what might they have been? Searches of the many websites dedicated to the missions of Bomber Command yielded a few fragments. His service number was easy to find, and I knew already that he flew in 625 Squadron, based at Kelstern in Lincolnshire.

And a long way down one page, below an almost indecipherable list of names, acronyms, ranks and abbreviations, there was this:

SGT DM BLACKMORE – (LATER P/O) DONALD M BLACKMORE, FLEW HIS 'SECOND-DICKIE' TRIP WITH W/O ASLETT TO BERLIN ON 2ND/3RD DECEMBER 1943 IN LANCASTER W4999. ON THEIR RETURN A CRASH LANDING SEVERELY DAMAGED THE AIRCRAFT AND B/A SGT JENNINGS SUSTAINED A BADLY BROKEN LEG. SGT GEOFF YATES FLEW IN HIS STEAD THEREAFTER IN BLACKMORE'S CREW.

The "second-dickie" trip was one in which a newly trained pilot was taken up with an experienced crew prior to captaining their own aircrew. It refers to the seat usually occupied by the Flight Engineer, who, though not a pilot,

Above:
Pilot Officer
John
McDonough,
probably taken
in 1944

Right: An Avro
Lancaster II
pictured in
flight on 26
August 1943,
as the bombing
campaign was
nearing its
height

could fly the plane in the event of calamity. In this case, the trip was basically work experience for my father among the flak, fighters and fury above Berlin.

This flight, with its mercifully untragic end, was sufficiently notable to earn another account on a site recording missions flown from Lincolnshire:

> CODED CF-G, AIRBORNE 1650 2ND DEC FROM KELSTERN. RETURNED TO BASE AND WHILE PREPARING TO LAND BOTH PORT ENGINES CUT, CAUSING AN IMMEDIATE CRASH-LANDING AT 2350 DURING WHICH THE LANCASTER COLLIDED WITH AN OBSTRUCTION AND WAS WRECKED. NO INJURIES REPORTED. W/O ASLETT, SGT BOTT AND SGT COOPER TRANSFERRED TO PFF AND WERE KILLED, TOGETHER, 23RD APR 44, DURING OPERATIONS TO LAON. SEE; ND592. W/O P.R.ASLETT, SGT D.M.BLACKMORE, SGT J.W.BOTT, SGT H.B.COOPER, SGT C.L.JENNINGS, F/S R.A.VERRY, P/O R.O.BUDD, SGT E.B.THOMAS.

No broken leg in this account but a grim forecast for three of my father's crewmates. Reality begins to intrude upon schoolboy fantasy.

My friend, Peter McDonough, more of whom later, had pointed me towards the Operations Record Books (ORBS) for 625 Squadron: hundreds of individual pages listing every mission and crew member. These have not been digitised, so studying them involves painstakingly opening every page to read the dense typescript.

Here I found that two days before Christmas that same year, on what must have been one of his first flights as pilot and captain, there was another mishap on a mission to Berlin. Two hours after taking off, his Lancaster jettisoned its bomb load in what turned out to be the mistaken belief that one of its engines was on fire. A mild reproach was attached to the debriefing note: "Disappointing – inexperienced crew." It's not clear whether my father is making that point or is the object of the criticism.

I could find no further such disappointments in the ORBs and apart from a gradually increasing impatience with the Pathfinder Force (PFF), who lit the bombers' path, most of my father's observations to the debrief officer are factual accounts of missions that seem to have been largely successful. On one occasion, he describes a mission to Berlin in which the defenders seemed indifferent to their attackers as "Rather a pleasant trip" – something I can almost hear him saying.

These accounts, preserved on fading paper, are deceptively dull, recording the squadron's not quite nightly raids in stark and unemotional language, even when a plane has to make an emergency landing or crew members have to be taken to hospital after being injured by flak or fighter fire. Every now and again a flight will be listed with its crew and take-off recorded but with a stark DID NOT RETURN typed in capitals in the space left for details.

The facts for bomber crew over the course of the war make shocking reading: of 125,000 aircrew, more than 57,000 were killed, another 8,400 were injured and nearly 10,000 found themselves prisoners of war. In other words, a crew member had a better than even chance of being a casualty (killed, injured or imprisoned). And barely an even chance of not being killed. For comparison, an infantryman in the trenches in the Great War had only a one in seven chance of being killed.

Max Hastings, in his new book on the Dambusters raid, *Chastise*, writes of Lancaster crews: "The fliers might spend seven or eight months at a given station, but would more plausibly vanish over Germany, some night or other. In the spring of 1943, less than one man in five was completing a thirty-trip tour of operations, and only 2.5 per cent finished a second tour. No crew is recorded as having offered to Sir Arthur Harris the old Roman gladiators' farewell to the emperor, Morituri te salutamus – We who are about to die salute you – but that was the way things were."

My father completed two tours.

And then there is the other side of this bitter equation to consider. Official estimates put the number of civilians killed by the Allied bombing campaign between 300,000 and 600,000. These days there seems little doubt that what were promulgated as strategic bombing raids on military targets were much less discriminate. In particular, the raids on Hamburg in 1943 (45,000 dead) and Dresden (25,000) in 1945 are troubling to the modern, liberal conscience.

I recall with exquisitely painful regret, as a teenager at an adult dinner party, once confronting my father about Dresden. I had just read Kurt Vonnegut's Slaughterhouse-Five and was full of righteous indignation at the firestorm that killed so many so late in the war. My father met my ill-informed outburst with a stony passivity that must have strengthened his lifelong determination not to speak of such things to me.

His silence on the subject only confirmed my glib assumption that he had taken part, but I could not find his name and crew in the ORB flight lists for 625 Squadron for the Dresden raid. I doubt he would have thought that made the slightest difference to his culpability or otherwise. He didn't get to choose his missions, after all, and in any case I never sensed he doubted the justice of the bombing campaign.

≈≈≈≈≈≈

Last September I travelled to Lincolnshire with my friend, Peter McDonough. We had met more than 40 years earlier, as teachers at a school in Kent. His father, John, was still in the RAF then and, by one of life's small coincidences, had also served in 625 Squadron during the war. John was five years younger than my father – a giant chasm in experience then – and neither of them could remember meeting the other. It is possible that they were never stationed there at the same time but it pleases me to imagine them passing each other on their daily rounds at Kelstern, 30 years before their sons, entirely by chance, would become lasting friends.

Peter had arranged for us to be shown around the Lincolnshire Aviation Heritage Centre at East Kirkby and to be given a tour of one of only two functioning Lancasters in the country. Avro Lancaster NX611, or Just Jane, as East Kirkby's star attraction is known, has been painstakingly restored by the Panton family to something like her original glory, as a memorial to a beloved son and brother, Christopher, who died in a mission over Nuremberg in 1944. Jane may no longer be able to fly but she can still trundle around the huge runway at a surprising lick.

Our first surprise was the number of people who had turned up to see her that day. The school holidays were long over and East Kirkby is by no means an easy place to reach by public transport. Yet everywhere there were visitors, a good many younger than Peter and I, who had come to see this mighty fragment of the past.

Our second surprise was finding that just being the sons of wartime aircrew brought us an undeserved but apparently real deference from anyone who happened to become aware of who we were.

We joined the crowd to watch as the quartet of mighty Rolls-Royce Merlin 24s thundered into life. It was impossible not to smile as Jane rumbled down the runway once more.

When she had taxied back into position, we were taken aboard. Wartime aircraft like the Spitfire, Hurricane, even the Mosquito or Halifax, seem to attract devotion in people much too young ever to have seen them in meaningful action. But the Lancaster attracts affection like no other.

The staff steering us round that narrow cramped fuselage were mostly ex-servicemen and women, full of reverence for Jane and all she represented. They took us first to the rear-gun turret. Here the "Tail-end Charlie" would strap himself in, closing two metal doors behind his back (so the plane could still fly if he was blown into the night), his crotch pressed painfully against an iron bar for the duration of the flight – perhaps eight hours or more. His parachute, by the way, hung from a hook back inside the fuselage. Temperatures might drop to minus 40 Celsius but his glass box was unheated and if he needed the toilet, well, you know.

We made our way along the fuselage, clambering over the large impediment of the wing spar, posed for pictures in the space occupied by the mid-upper gunner, edged past the navigator's table where the wireless operator might also have worked, peered down at the bomb aimer's gloomy hole, paused at that second-dickie perch and, next to it, on

Donald Blackmore (second from left, front row) and what was almost certainly one of his crews in 1943

the left, the pilot's seat. We sat where our fathers would have done: me in the pilot's seat, Peter on that second dickie. We posed for pictures, leaning out of the cockpit, thumbs up, and thought of our fathers as the former RAF pilot who was our guide explained why so few who sat there ever escaped if their plane was badly damaged: the pilot, who was invariably also the captain of the aircraft, was under orders to be the last to leave, to keep the plane steady for the others.

And then we made our way slowly back through the obstacle course of the fuselage. Our guide pointed out what should have been obvious: it was a tricky business negotiating that narrow passage partly lit, with the plane at a standstill, and would have been even had we been 40 years younger. Imagine doing it in the dark, he remarked casually, perhaps while also being badly injured but certainly frozen and frightened, with a parachute on your back, and enemies outside shooting at you. Oh yes, and with the plane on fire and plunging earthwards from 20,000 feet.

The citation for that DFC remains elusive and not only because wartime records, especially for the RAF it seems, are still in some disarray, at least for a researcher like me used to the lazy short-cut of the search engine. But a bigger impediment might have been the creeping realisation that I might not really want to find it, after all. Perhaps that medal was awarded for a single gallant act or flight. Perhaps it was for completing two tours of operations. Perhaps for something else altogether.

In any case, I had climbed into that Lancaster hoping to know my father a little better and found something he had deliberately kept from me. Fear.

I closed my eyes in that narrow, dark tube and felt for a fraction of a second the engulfing terror that my father and his crewmates and many like them must have had to overcome night after night after night. No DFC could do justice to that.

We emerged from Just Jane into the cool sunlight of a glorious early autumn day. I found myself wondering what my youthful father would have made of this scene. Dad would have laughed, I think, at the idea that this elderly gent, descending so gingerly from the fuselage, was his son. He would, I'm certain, have been glad to know he had defied those terrible odds to survive the war and have children. And I hope, too, that he would have felt a swell of pride that he had managed to give me everything he'd had to do without: a home, an education, an example, a father. ⌒.

Sqd Ldr Donald McKenzie Blackmore DFC, pilot, was born 21 October 1919 and died 8 January 1998

The squadron leader (with the author) some time in 1957, as his RAF career was drawing to a close

KNOCK, KNOCK. WHO'S THERE?

Stand-up comedy is overwhelmingly male and seriously lacking in diversity. *Susie Walker* finds trying to break into it as a woman is no laughing matter

A FEMALE COMEDIAN

I decided to become a stand-up comic. I know, right. What is wrong with me? About two years ago, something shifted. I realised I had something to say and felt ready to say it. If you are thinking it was a mid-30s existential crisis you'd be absolutely right. It dawned on me that my jokes were wasted at the weekly operations meeting. It had become too easy for me to bat back heckles from the chief financial officer. I needed to be playing to bigger rooms.

It turns out the grass roots of comedy hasn't changed in decades. Stand-up remains blissfully unencumbered by the democratising forces of self-publishing that have liberated female writing talent. There is still just the one grim route to making it big in comedy. Metaphorically and literally, it's a dark path – not just because it takes place mainly underground. At night.

Amateur comedy is still a hostile environment for women. Comedy, like advertising, doesn't just reflect culture. It shapes it too. Being an amateur female stand-up is like being stuck inside a bad joke.

It is true that women are becoming slowly more visible in comedy. There are more female comedians on television and landing UK tours. I'm thrilled for Aisling Bea, Roisin Conaty and London Hughes, I really am, but Chortle's database shows that only 18 per cent of comics working professionally are women.

Being a female stand-up is brutal. You're going to have to want it bad: more than getting enough sleep; more than spending time with loved ones; certainly more than only using toilets with soap and a working lock on the door. And yet, in spite of it all, stand-up has been one of the highlights of my life. So if anyone is still tempted, here is my handy guide to Making It As A Female Stand-up.

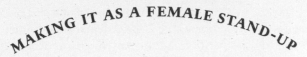

MAKING IT AS A FEMALE STAND-UP

WHEN YOU COME OUT AS A STAND-UP, YOU'RE COMING OUT AS A NEEDY CLOWN

First, you need to have something to say. Doesn't matter what, or why. Believing you of all people have something to say to Other People is the first step. Accept that you'll think you've gone mad. Telling yourself things are absolutely fine and completely normal when they're morally dubious and very unusual is part of the comedic life. Then you need to pluck up the courage to do something about it. In my case this took six months. When you come out as a stand-up, you're coming out as a needy clown. Accept it, own it, move on.

WELCOME TO COMEDY. GLAMOROUS ISN'T IT?

The jury's out on whether it's better to be taught or to launch yourself cold into the brutality of the open mic circuit. There's no way I would have had the confidence to do it without training wheels. Maddie Campion, another gigging stand-up, told me: "I regret not doing a course when I started because I got loads of bad advice from men who ran open mics, which I think meant a lot of people saw me be utter shit in my first year."

Doing an introduction to stand-up course is a rite of passage. Logan Murray's, which I did, is regarded as one of if not the best. It has brilliant alumni (Diane Morgan,

Greg Davies, Andi Osho, Josh Widdicombe and the 2019 winner of Funny Women, the UK's only national women-only comedy competition, Laura Smyth) and a menacingly diligent, low-fi approach to marketing that convinced me to cough up the £500 course fee.

The content is a mash-up of how to generate material, improvisation, "the business" and the all-important mic craft. Mic[rophone] craft, which includes how to hold a mic, speak into a mic and move a mic stand and not get tangled up in the wires, is to stand-ups as smoking fags and drinking Jack Daniel's is to rock stars. Doing it well just makes you seem like you're legit.

So it was that one rainy Tuesday evening, I went to a run-down university tower block in London Bridge. Welcome to comedy. Glamorous isn't it?

EVERYONE SEEMS TO BE RECOVERING FROM SOMETHING

There were 16 people on my course. Most were shifty-looking men. Everyone seemed to be recovering from something: from mental illness to redundancy to divorce. We were like an attention-seekers anonymous group. From the first exercise, the men were more confident, more sure of their material, more comfortable critiquing that of others and offering advice. The women were self-conscious, sometimes cripplingly so. But I felt at home in this crowd of weird, interesting people. I was hooked. I didn't have to compensate, I could just be myself. Comedy, like all the writing disciplines, is a lonely task but some of the people I met on the course are now good friends.

COMEDIANS CAN BE
REALLY WEIRD

The course ends with a "showcase" – your first five-minute set, performed for an invited audience of family and friends. I took the day off work to prepare. I drilled and drilled my material, remembering the notes I'd been given: slow down, listen to the audience, take in the whole room, relax. Relax! Sure, I'll relax. I mean, OK COOL TOTALLY RELAXED NOW. I was put 13th on a bill of 16. There's the relaxation right there. Two solid hours of pure torture. I paced around outside the venue in Baltic winds without a coat trying to slow my breathing. Sidebar: one of my course mates used some of her precious five minutes of stage time to troll me personally. Comedians really can be weird. To my absolute astonishment, my set went brilliantly.

FANCY INTERIORS ARE NOT DE RIGUEUR
IN AMATEUR COMEDY

If you survive your first gig, you've got to face another. And another. There's 300-400 open mic nights every week in London, so finding a gig to perform at is another world of admin. To help, there are shared Google Maps and spreadsheets, email notification forums, closed Facebook groups and tips from other comedians. My favourite nights are TNT in Kentish Town, organised by the charming Sarma Woolf; the line-up and energy are unfailingly good. G&B, run and MC'd by the brilliant Kyle Wallace, was described to me once as the most "woke" comedy night in London. But my advice is try a few to see where you fit in.

The business model of open mic nights remains a

mystery. You won't get paid, and nobody pays to come and watch you. There's the bar money, sometimes a raffle, quite often some ropey merch. Can it really all hang on the content of the bucket shaken on the door at the end?

No two gigs have the same booking process. The rules, the rules. There are so many rules. Often a gig will have a set of aggressively specific but wilfully vague and changeable rules. If you don't follow them you can (and will) be barred from performing. If you have to cancel, you'll be barred. If you're late, you'll be barred. If you don't follow the rules of how to book a spot in the first place, you'll be barred. One of the most important rules is that no matter when you perform, you MUST stay at the gig until the final act has performed. If you don't do this? Sorry, you're barred.

The majority of gigs are "bringers". A bringer is a gig where you're only allowed on stage if you bring someone with you. If you don't bring someone, you won't be going on stage. And you might get barred. To get the kind of stage time you need to improve, you need plenty of friends (or a dutiful partner) happy to silently drink themselves through an evening of possibly terrible comedy several times a week.

When you get to the gig, do not expect to find helpful information about, for example, when you might expect to be on stage, how you might find out when you're required on stage, or how long you might have to be at the venue. Through trial and error, I have developed a cast-iron approach: arrive early and sit quietly.

Oh, and you must not bring your own food or drinks. Seriously. BYO is considered the height of rudeness in amateur comedy, an anarchic move. If you really have to eat, buy crisps.

Some of the people you'll meet backstage include the hipster twenty-somethings with a romanticised, faux beatnik notion of the scene. Their material includes talking to their succulents, VEGANISM, being socially awkward and obviously, duh, dating. Then there are those with anxiety and depression (any age), people for whom doing stand-up is wincingly difficult but wildly affirming and cathartic. There are comedians of the school I like to call "European Quirks", who are having a whale of a time post-Brexit. Their material is based around miscommunication gags, adjusting-to-London-life lolz and how stag-dos are ruining their home towns. You will also meet retired men who do entire sets of cringe-yourself-to-death puns and oblivious 1970s sexism.

Most pubs have a damp, weird, noisy, poorly lit (or eye-wateringly bright) function room tucked away somewhere in which they run one comedy one night a week. Fancy interiors are not de rigueur in amateur comedy. As a wannabe stand-up, you'll be frequenting venues that may feature some or all of the following crimes against interior design: damp; fluorescent strip lighting or no lighting at all; a tacky floor or a wet floor; yellowing or inexplicably wet walls; boarded-up windows, chicken wire over windows or simply no windows; access routes that wouldn't withstand a council health and safety inspection; and toilets so cold you have to put your coat back on to use them.

At one gig I was kettled backstage for almost three hours with nine other acts. Backstage was the corridor that joined the hotel kitchen to the upstairs restaurant. I worried about the plates of lasagne and nachos travelling at speed beneath a ceiling caked in black mould.

COMEDY IS A MASOCHIST'S GAME

Failing, like mindfulness, is very on trend but failing in comedy is nothing other than pain. Awful, excruciating pain. And it will happen to you, over and over. Comedians are odd-shaped people. You have to be comfortable with being extremely vulnerable. You can't be cocky; you can't be arrogant; anyone can die (on stage) at any moment. Then you have to be able it back down with a drink after to reflect objectively. It's a real leveller. You must develop an objective and multidimensional approach to analyse why and how you smashed a gig or totally bombed.

Superstition is your friend if it means you can keep gigging. It's important to remain on high alert – the tiniest thing can distract you. Being tired, hot, hungry, thirsty, late, receiving an unexpected text message, not knowing the material well enough or knowing it too well can all spell disaster. I threw away a whole outfit following a horrible gig because I decided an aggravating factor was that the sleeves made me feel weird.

And those are just the things you can control. The MC might be terrible. The chair layout might create an unsettling energy. Maybe the act before you was just too brilliant – that's a dead-cert for bombing. There could be someone in the audience laughing too loud (sounds strange, but this does happen). The audience might be cold. Or there might be no audience at all.

But when you get a gig that goes well, it's incredible. It's more than affirming. The adrenalin is extreme. It is a wild privilege to share your take on the world with a group of people who laugh along in recognition.

Do whatever you need to do to recover. You are taken

more seriously when you've netted 100 gigs and there's a trope that if you just keep going you'll make it after seven years. So after nursing your wounded ego, get back on it. Repeat steps 4-7 up to 500 times until you either give up or make it.

As for me, I've now done about 40 gigs. In my first year or so, I made the semi-finals of Amused Moose National New Comic competition and the quarter-finals in Funny Women. I haven't yet gigged outside London, partly because I don't have a car and partly because I also have a quite demanding full-time job. Venturing beyond Zone 3 is next on my agenda.

RESIGNED DISAPPOINTMENT AND SHEER RAGE

Comedy is the crucible of identity politics and free speech, where raw, ill-advised remarks and clumsy cultural observations bubble in a cauldron of resigned disappointment and sheer rage. The fact that everyone is laughing (on a good day, at least) doesn't make it any less important.

The demographic at the amateur level is largely millennial white men; between 70-100 per cent of pretty much every gig I've ever done or seen. The material ranges from witty takes on modern life to sensitive self-reflection to whole sets of one-liners (really guys?) and tone-deaf anger. I watched one act smash up the mic stand, a chair and a table in a tiny venue with a front row full of women "as an experiment". Sure.

Turns out misogyny is alive and well on the stand-up circuit. I've sat through several "ironic" rape jokes, a call to bring back witch-burning and relentless low-level sexism. It wouldn't be so bad if this sort of material didn't go down so well. There are brilliant promoters who have clear guidelines on what material is acceptable, but they are the exception. More often than not, people of colour, LGBTQ+ acts, older people (especially older women) and people with disabilities are massively underrepresented.

Female comics are conspicuously absent too. They were either never there to begin with or they've given up. They're at work, looking after kids, or battling the Universal Credit labyrinth. Gigging three evenings a week for no money just isn't feasible for most of us. Many are put off by fears for their personal safety. Nobody covers your travel costs so most have to use public transport. Walking down empty streets in dodgy parts of town at 11.30pm is not safe. In 2018, the Australian comedian Eurydice Dixon was raped and murdered on her way home from a gig in Melbourne. There is no comedy union to protect comedians, no code of conduct, no shared information about incidents. According to industry press Chortle, one in four female comedians in the UK has been molested.

I have been the only woman in a 20-person line-up more than once. The gender imbalance in the line-up is reflected in the audience. One begets the other because when you're playing to a room full of men some jokes just don't land as well. Edgy and even friendly feminism is met with taut, awkward silence and blank stares. The comedians who "make it" are all pushed through this narrow talent funnel – the people who book you and the people you perform for. I want to smash things up when I see the next hotly tipped female comedian's

material is all dick jokes and watered-down feminism.
But I get why it happens.

HEARING A TON OF DIFFERENT FEMALE PERSPECTIVES IN ONE NIGHT IS EXHILARATING

I feel like a minority doing stand-up. It's uncomfortable and unnerving to be so outnumbered. And it's worse for people of colour. There's a handful of nights that showcase and support working-class comedians, female comedians, LGBTQ+ comedians and comedians of colour but they're only once every few months. Funny Women's Time of the Month, G&B Girlpower, FOC it Up and Sikisa aka Twix's Stand Up 4 Women are all great nights to catch a diverse line-up. I've had some of my best gigs in women-only line-ups. Hearing a ton of different female perspectives in one night is exhilarating and refreshing. Tear-jerking, even.

Don't get me wrong, there's plenty about the circuit that I love. Seeing acts before they're mainstream is like being let in on a brilliant secret. Watching (or doing) amateur comedy will unceremoniously yank you out of your echo chamber. Truly, I recommend it.

But the game seems rigged at all levels of the industry. Backstage, it's the dark ages (or at least the late 80s). Which is ironic when the work on stage hinges on being current and vital. I have come to accept and understand that it takes seven years (seven years!) to make it as a comedian. It's a cryptically complex craft that yields results only from sheer bloody-minded resilience. Can I face seven years of damp basements, late nights and rape jokes to make it? It's the only way. 🔈

Water

torture

The anatomy of a flood
By Simon Barnes

he flood did not begin with the rain. It started long, long before the first drop fell. You could say, I suppose, that it began with the way the glaciers shaped the countryside below Wenlock Edge, creating the steep valleys that gather and concentrate the water with such devastating efficiency.

But you can't just blame the last Ice Age for the troubles of the 21st Century, for the ferocious waters that smashed down a bridge in the town of Ludlow a dozen miles downstream in 2007 and killed a retired maths teacher called Mike Ellis in 2012. If you go up to the source of the River Corve in Shropshire and start to travel down, bit by bit, you might come to the conclusion that humans had spent the last couple of thousand years doing all they could to make sure that flooding takes place as often and as disastrously as possible.

Ah, how lovely it looks: a thin, busy trickle of Bourton Brook heading down the dale, the source of the mighty Corve just a hundred yards away. We humans respond to water with great warmth: how could we not? Water is life, and the sight of water, moving past us, in a brook or a river, soothes us to our very souls. The great lords built their country houses and then dug a lake before them, to please the eye of those that lived within. Water is home: we can't permanently live anywhere unless we have a good deal of the stuff.

And yet water kills, and does so with great efficiency. It also destroys the works of humanity with immense regularity. We build beside rivers and streams because we need the water they bring us, but then, when there is too much of a good thing, the water changes from invaluable friend to implacable enemy. First we need the stuff, then we can't wait to get rid of it. This is a contradiction at the heart of human life, and it has dictated water policy across the centuries.

iann Scriven, from Alveley, near Bridgnorth, was also affected by the Shropshire floods of 2007. After the landscape around their house was devastated, she said: "Before, it was a lovely idyllic place with a lovely babbling brook." Brooks are good at babbling, but every now and then they roar. Flooding and flood management costs the country an annual £2.2 billion; the average insurance claim for each flooded house is £30,000.

The shattering floods that hit Ludlow and the villages between the town and Wenlock Edge began not in the town, but upstream, in the network of babbling brooks that feed the Corve, and in the river as it moves down towards its confluence with the Teme in Ludlow; the Teme then flows into the Severn, which reaches the sea in the Bristol Channel.

And while the last Ice Age made its contribution, it

was the human management of the landscape that made the flooding of Ludlow and its surrounding villages inevitable. Across the centuries we have – in some cases quite literally – paved the way for the rain, directing it and guiding it in ways that might have been designed to cause us maximum inconvenience.

It begins with deforestation. Trees hold water and inhibit the flow of water; a wood releases the water slowly into the landscape below. But humans across the world and throughout history have taken away the trees, to use the wood, initially for building houses – Ludlow itself is a fine town filled with impressive timber-framed houses – and for ships and for fuel and for a million other good reasons.

The clearing of land opens it up for agriculture, and Shropshire is a rural county that is centred on farming, both arable and livestock. Both kinds of farming require water, but not too much of it.

So the land is drained; managed so that much of the water that falls on the field is not held there, but released quickly, into field drains and thence into the watercourses. When water falls in any quantity, it is important for the farmer to get rid of it as quickly as possible. It runs off beneath the surface of the land and enters brooks, streams and rivers.

If you keep domestic livestock on a pasture – and in the past half-century we are grazing five times as much stock as we used to – the earth gets compacted. It then becomes less able to absorb water.

In such cases the water also runs off the top, and does so especially at times of high rainfall, flowing downhill to be concentrated in the watercourses.

Now for the watercourses themselves. We like to think of babbling brooks and sweetly flowing rivers as entirely the work of nature, but that is not the case at all. There is not a river and scarcely a stream in this country that runs truly wild. Across history, we have reorganised them, reshaped them, straightened them, dug them deeper, all of which makes them more efficient at getting rid of water quickly.

You don't want the problems of excess water, so you get rid of it as fast as possible, and let them deal with it downstream. The people downstream have exactly the same attitude to their own much greater problem. And so the people still further downstream... have their bridges and their houses and sometimes their inhabitants swept away.

The bed of a free-flowing stream – before being reorganised by humans – is likely to be broad and flat, with no trees or other obstructions in the middle. In other words, in the drier summer months it makes a damn good road, for people, for livestock and for carts, the small flow in the middle far from inconvenient. The secondary function of the streambed later became its primary function: it was the road. The stream was allowed to flow alongside, in a channel deepened and straightened by the hands and spades of humanity: as you can see, for example, in the village of Brockton.

Later, these adopted roads were paved; they now carry the transport on which we all depend. And if there is anything that water likes, it's a hard, smooth, sloping

Flood plains

Humans use floodplains to grow crops and graze cattle, inhibiting the river from naturally soaking the landscape.

Brockton

Wenlock Edge

Diddlebury

Culmington

Deforestation

As trees hold water, a wood releases the water slowly into the landscape below.

Farming

Water is drained from land so that it is not held on the field but released quickly into field drains and from there, into the watercourses.

Livestock

Keeping livestock on a pasture compacts the earth, making it less able to absorb water.

Storms

Climate change adds more energy into the weather system in the form of heat, making storms more frequent and more dramatic.

Ludlow

The causes of the Ludlow flood

Stanton Lacy

River Corve

River Teme

Roads

Drainage capacity can struggle with large amounts of water which flows down roads at an immense pace.

121

surface, down which it can flow at immense pace. We have created a network of such opportunities. And that's what happens below Wenlock Edge when the rain falls thick and heavy. When a sudden drastic summer downpour dumps its myriad gallons on the countryside, the streams and brooks and rivers resume their former courses and race downstream, the blacktop roads becoming faster than the mill-races that once played an important part in the local economy.

Then there are the villages, like Diddlebury, historically built along those helpful streams and rivers that make life possible. Of course, no one wants a rambling, free-flowing river on their doorstep, so the waterways were organised with still more determination and purpose, pushed into hard, straight, narrow channels that flow most pleasingly past the chocolate-box cottages.

In the village of Culmington there is a classic example of such management: the river, passing under a narrow road bridge that speeds it up in times of spate, is then forced into a sharp right turn by means of a brick wall. This is what is known as a choke-point: a place where, in times of very high flow, the water is gathered together to become a crisis.

R ivers flood, it's only natural. Sometimes there is more water than usual, but unusual events are part of routine. That's why rivers create floodplains: the places where the river routinely spreads itself out luxuriously and soaks the landscape, sometimes for miles, before flowing away as time passes and the rains stop. It's a wholly natural phenomenon.

But floodplains, flat and fecund, also offer priceless opportunities for humans to grow crops and graze cattle. We don't want the floodplains for the rivers, we want them so we can make food. So all over Corve Dale, the river has been cut off from its floodplains: the fields drained, the river embanked, canalised and straightened. It's a pattern repeated across the country.

In other words, the system, established in an ad-hoc way through the centuries, is designed to get rid of water as fast as possible. And that is why, in 2007, the Burway Bridge in Ludlow was washed away by the water we were getting rid of. It was described as a once-in-200-years event, and on those grounds there was an application for a housing project on the former floodplain of the Rivers Corve and Teme in Ludlow. It never happened: in 2012 there was another once-in-200-years event, the one that did for the poor maths teacher.

It's a fact that extreme weather events have become normal. Many readers will remember the BBC weatherman, Michael Fish, who reported that a viewer had expressed fears that there was a hurricane on the way. "Don't worry, there isn't," he said cheerfully. In that night's Great Storm of 1987, 18 people died. Such dramatic events have since been accepted as routine abnormalities.

It makes perfect sense: if you put more energy into a system, it becomes more energetic. Thanks to climate change we have put a great deal more energy into the weather system, in the form of heat. Major storms are now more frequent and more dramatic. So, having for centuries created a system in which occasional flooding is inevitable

– there was serious flooding of the Corve in 1886, 1924, 1927 and 1946 before the events of 2007 and 2012 – we have now created a weather system that makes extreme events more frequent and more violent.

All of which left me standing under a bridge at Stanton Lacy, three miles north of Ludlow, looking for signs of otter. We found them too. Otters like to lay down their spraint – droppings – in prominent places under bridges, for these tokens are full of information useful to others of their kind. Above, a migrating party of 100 house martins called and hawked for insects. Luke Neal, deputy manager of the rivers team at the Shropshire Wildlife Trust, was turning over stones in the middle of the stream looking for white-clawed crayfish. He found one, too. It's a species battling back against pollution and the presence of the introduced American signal crayfish. Under the carriageway above us was a dipper's nest.

All that adds up to good evidence that the river here is in good shape for wildlife. And that has a great deal more to do with the disaster of downstream flooding than you might think.

There have been a lot of anti-flooding measures established by the Environment Agency. But perhaps the most effective part of this spend has been £40,000 a year capital spend that goes to the Shropshire Wildlife Trust.

Luke Neal, deputy manager of the rivers team at the Shropshire Wildlife Trust, with one of the woody debris barriers built on the Wilde Brook – one of the tributaries of the River Corve – in and effort to reduce the risk of flooding

Neal took me on a tour of these measures. The brooks and streams that reach the Corve have been punctuated again and again with what are officially termed woody debris barriers. They are more easily understood as leaky dams. The fish can get through them; so can the water, just not so fast.

They are gloriously like the dams we made as children: woods and branches across the stream, handy trees to secure them and handfuls of brash to patch the holes. A sequence of them descending a slope, steep or gentle, causes the water to slow down, back up, create deep, still pools in which classic stream vegetation is now making a comeback; these are punctuated by occasional fast, shallow, oxygenating riffles that bring life back into the water.

All this enriches the river, makes it more natural and more full of life, precisely the brief of any wildlife organisation. But it also slows the flow of the water, and makes flooding downstream less likely and less catastrophic. A lot of small natural devices are overcoming the work and traditions of centuries. Keep the water, hold on to it and then release it slowly. Better for otter and crayfish, better for the residents of Ludlow.

You could see the pride and delight flowing from Neal as we walked the streams and brooks and surveyed the dams: simple technology that has been road-tested or rather river-tested in the United States.

Flood prevention is the aim, wildlife the inevitable bonus. Elsewhere, he showed me ponds that have been dug, with a simple barrier designed to help it hold more water in times of flood. There are other measures that include the creation of swales in steep hillsides: basically a series of hollowed-out steps that hold the water as it descends the hillsides.

All this requires sympathetic landowners; as always, there are some enthusiasts and some stubborn hold-outs. It helps that the National Trust owns a large property towards the headwaters called Wilderhope Manor, formerly owned by John Cadbury, the chocolate manufacturer. The Trust has taken on the catchment-based river project and established Wilderhope as something of a template project. The work and its results are measured and monitored by the University of Cardiff; the efficacy of these simple measures will soon have the numbers to go with it. The university is also creating laboratory models of flood projects.

There are limits to what you can do with a small sum of money, but Neal has also been able to plant 9,000 trees and established 1.25 kilometres of hedges as further holding measures, with finance from the Woodland Trust and 10:10, the climate change charity. A further possibility, one that would be likely to polarise opinion, would be the release of beavers, which have been shown to be the best upstream flood managers of all. Eurasian beavers were once widespread in this country and there are now established populations in Devon and along the River Tay in Scotland.

It is a beguilingly simple format: a mixture of low tech and clear thinking, one that saves millions of pounds downstream. And what's more, it works. The industrial solutions like concrete barriers and deep dredging do matter – but these natural solutions are a deeply effective shift to a better use of both land and money.

In previous times agricultural subsidies encouraged upland farmers to overstock their land, usually with sheep, to graze them low, dry them out and compact them, so causing water to run off them at pace. Field drainage and ditch-digging was also heavily subsidised. In other words, we were subsidising farmers to cause flooding.

There are at least possibilities of running the land on a more rational basis. The post-EU plans for such subsidies, under the Environmental Land Management schemes, are predicated on the slogan of "public money for public good". Or, to put that another way, what's good for otters and crayfish is good for the people of Britain – especially if you happen to live in Ludlow. ⌒•

MELTING

Disko Bay ——— • Jakobshavn glacier

GREENLAND

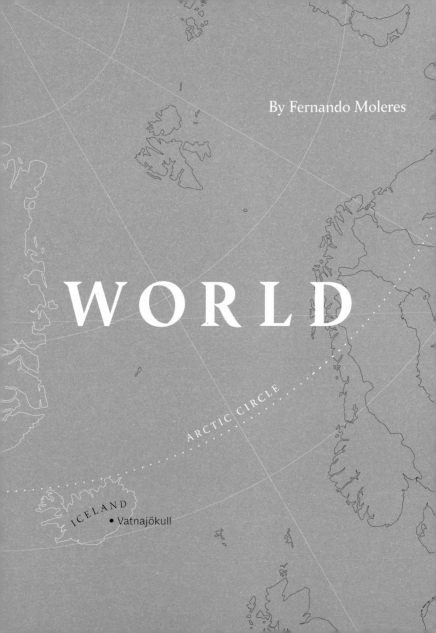

By Fernando Moleres

WORLD

ARCTIC CIRCLE

ICELAND
• Vatnajökull

Fernando Moleres has spent much of his career as a photographer capturing the injustices of child labour around the world. From 2014–15 the Spaniard turned his attention to an even greater threat to the next generation: climate change. He travelled to Greenland and Iceland to highlight the impact of global warming. His "Melting Landscapes" project gives the vastness of the Arctic a minimalist treatment, emphasising its vulnerability and showing, in his words, the "hardness and, at the same time, the fragility of the Arctic".

Icebergs floating in Disko Bay, north-west Greenland, having broken off from the Jakobshavn glacier. One of its icebergs is said to have hit the 'Titanic'

Covering an area of more than 3,000 square miles, which is 8 per cent of the country, Vatnajökull, in the south-east of Iceland, is the largest glacier in Europe. In parts it is more than half a mile thick but, like so many glaciers, it is in retreat, said to be melting at a rate of a metre per year. Vatnajökull contains Iceland's most active volcano, Grímsvötn

Two forlorn
icebergs
float through
the Ilulissat
Icefjord towards
Disko Bay in
Greenland. They
come from the
Jakobshavn
glacier,
Greenland's
largest. The
country holds
10 per cent of
the world's fresh
water in its ice
fields. If that
all melted, sea
levels would rise
by more than
7.5 metres

Jonathan Cake spent the summer playing Coriolanus in Central Park and found, much to his surprise and delight, that New York totally got Shakespeare's last great tragic hero

ACTING THE HARD MAN

Opening night at the Delacorte Theater in New York

My kids are riding on an alarmingly vertiginous Airbnb rope swing and I find myself hissing at them:

"You common cry of curs, whose breath I hate
As reek of the rotten fens, whose loves I prize
As the dead carcasses of unburied men
That do corrupt my air, I BANISH YOU!"

The kids are used to me talking like this to them, not just because of my spring-break gyp, far from our California bubble and anything unfried, on a road trip through Confederate flag-waving MAGA country, but because I'm brushing up my Coriolanus. Shakespeare's final tragedy is about to be performed by the Public Theater, the latest offering in their famous Free Shakespeare in the Park festival, a summer tradition in New York as inherent to the city's identity as the US Open tennis, the Naked Cowboy in Times Square and Alec Baldwin punching a photographer. The Public wants me to play Coriolanus.

The last time they did it was precisely 40 years ago, with some hack called Morgan Freeman in the title role. Another journeyman called Denzel Washington played a spear-carrier. American theatres almost never perform this play. I'm thrilled by the offer. At the same time I'm worried that Morgan and Denzel know something I don't. That it's an unperformable play. That 40 years wasn't long enough to get the stink out of the theatre. I suddenly feel like my daughter on the rope swing, thrilled by the height but nauseated by the possibility of falling. I suddenly feel like shoving her to one side, jumping on the rope swing ("Not of a woman's tenderness to be/ Requires nor child, nor woman's face to see./ I have sat too long"). And then, when I'm sailing high above the Tennessee ground, letting go.

> "Pluto and hell!
> All hurt behind! Backs red, and faces pale
> With flight and agued fear!"

A broken limb or two should see me safely through the summer and away from any onstage humiliation, the pain and memory of which would surely last much longer.

Instead I turn and look at the Tennessee backwoods and consider that when *Coriolanus* was first performed for James I – and scrutinised with quill-withering attention for signs of potential offence to the monarch – the invasion and pillage of this new world had just begun. Jamestown, the settlement that bore his name, had been established in neighbouring Virginia just a year or two before and a hell unleashed on the indigenous people of this country as unforgiving as anything imagined by *Coriolanus*:

> "...to ravish your own daughters and
> To melt the city leads upon your pates,
> To see your wives dishonour'd to your noses...
> Your temples burned in their cement..."

I abandon my children to the watertight Airbnb disclaimer, walk back inside and take the part.

TOPANGA CANYON
CALIFORNIA

Grey cloud is sluicing the Santa Monica Mountains outside. My mind is doing something similar, drifting from the words I should be learning to anxiety about getting myself extremely fit for this role and its natural corollary – thoughts of muffins.

A text from Dominic Dromgoole, theatre and film director: "Rumour has it that you're having another pop at Old Grumpyboots." Dominic was the shiny new artistic director of Shakespeare's Globe in 2006 when he directed me as Coriolanus in the inaugural show of his regime. Thirteen years, two kids and a relocation to America later, I recall troublingly little about that production. Particularly, it turns out, the very many lines. For a taciturn man of action – "Yet oft/ When blows have made me stay/ I fled from words..." – he really does bang on.

Except I can remember that we talked a lot about Roy Keane, Manchester United's Irish midfield warrior, his stroppy walkout from the then recent World Cup ("Stick it up yer bollocks", as pithy as anything Coriolanus can conjure) and his pathological need to be contrary, so similar to the Roman:

"He seeks their hate with greater devotion than can render it him..."

And I remember I had a very cool death, stabbed and falling, rock-star style, into the yard of the Globe, among the standing punters unique to that theatre, then passed above the heads of the crowd.

I also remember being dismayed when Dominic insisted that I come back out after this show-stopping death to perform the traditional Elizabethan post-play jig. "Jig?!" I said. "Fucking jig? Tough guys don't jig!" Trust me, he reassured, the jig works.

I sheepishly emerged after the first preview, half-heartedly capering downstage in my pointy shoes. It was like Oasis coming on stage at Knebworth. Those Elizabethans – and Dominic Dromgoole – knew a thing or two about cathartic release.

I also remembered secretly feeling, at the age of 39, slightly too old for the part. Coriolanus is characterised as an overgrown boy, a man child, and his whole identity exudes a kind of electrical current of restless energy.

Shakespeare is indulgently unspecific about the ages of many of his tragic heroes. Richard Burbage, his original leading man and presumably the first Coriolanus, had already played the gone-to-seed Mark Antony by this time, heavy enough to have jokes made about it as Cleopatra tries to winch him up to her monument. And the theatre – particularly the 2,000 seats of the Delacorte in Central Park – is hardly a camera close-up.

But, still, 13 years older than that? Ah well, I reasoned, so much is made in the play of Coriolanus's scars, his almost fetishised "marks of merit, the wounds received for his country" and everyone's desire to gawp at them. For better or worse, I feel I have more scars to show the people.

Thirty of us are crowded around a slim, commanding figure in our rehearsal space, the Newman, largest of the three auditoriums at the Public. The commanding figure is still commanding despite playing with what appears to be a post-apocalyptic doll's house.

Daniel Sullivan, our director, is explaining his concept for the setting of this production, using the design model, the world of the play in miniature.

When Dan explains something, we all listen. He has directed Tom Hanks as Falstaff, Al Pacino as Shylock; he's the Yoda of New York theatre and Shakespeare in the Park in particular. So much so that he almost gave his life for it, falling down an open trap door on the Delacorte stage 12 years ago and sustaining horrific injuries. He was back directing in that theatre the next summer.

Dan's plan takes its cue from David Wallace-Wells's almost unendurable book *The Uninhabitable Earth*. Unendurable because the climate-ravaged vision of societal and economic breakdown it offers is so persuasive and yet so beautifully written. Dan's idea is that Shakespeare's play, which presents the moment that ancient Rome tries to transition from tribal violence (where Coriolanus thrives) to the first spasm of democracy (where he falls), can only find an equivalent in our future, the future that Wallace-Wells presents so vividly.

He wants the production to imagine a time, 80 or a hundred years from now, after a climate apocalypse has broken like a global typhoon and returned its survivors to a state akin to ancient Rome: a state in which famine, thirst and the need to kill or be killed predominate; a state of savagery in which the vague memory of democracy, of a social order based on something more than violence, is trying to make a comeback.

Grounding the play in such sheer desperation leaves us all silent. Performing it in the open air, in the middle of Manhattan, as today's city teems around us, feels deeply poignant. The air suddenly seems thicker, the screams of the sirens more alarming. It's rare that the stakes evoked by a theatre production are also the stakes of the audience. Dan could have set this play in, I don't know, 1890s Vienna, or the American Civil War, or any other abstract and an audience might have appreciated the parallels, but they wouldn't feel them, they can't tap into the anxiety we all feel about the present and the near future.

Like it or not, New York always feels like exhibit A in the disaster movies of our minds; it's why so many actual disaster movies are set there. The symbolically small island of Manhattan, which stands with all its life force for the whole world in our imaginations, is lashed by tsunamis, its canyons of skyscrapers reduced to rubble, its dense mass of humanity running like rats from the horror engulfing it. Imagining Shakespeare's Rome right here, among the debris of the city, feels all too easy.

A man as brave as Coriolanus, as dedicated to honour and virtue, could flourish in that debris. And then be lost when the city tries to rebuild its foundations and the foundations of care for everyone, however weak or afraid.

THE PUBLIC THEATER
NEW YORK CITY

I t's a stiflingly hot New York summer morning. I step into the mercifully air-conditioned foyer of the Public, mindful of what Wallace-Wells would say about the warming effects of A/C, to find a large group of people thronging the lobby. They appear to be playing a giant game of bingo. In fact they're calling the names of the winners of the raffle to get tickets for our show. Ah yes. An audience. Gulp. Although Shakespeare in the Park is free, the raffle winners won't have to queue all day in the boiling sun like everyone else. I keep my head down and head for the rehearsal room.

I'm early and inside, the auditorium is quiet. There is a lonely figure onstage, a lithe and elegant elderly gentleman performing a rigorous physical warm-up. This is Thomas Kopache, with a face off a Roman coin, five foot six of twisted cable, an ex-Navy serviceman, playing one of our Roman senators. Tom tells me he's been in this play before. He played Titus Lartius to Christopher Walken's Coriolanus in 1988.

I'm suddenly moved by the tracking of time in this profession. Lartius is the young buck soldier, a kind of sidekick to Coriolanus, in our production played by a wonderful actor in his early twenties called Chris Ghaffari, who's also my understudy. How was Walken's Coriolanus? "Hmm... eccentric." OK, good. "And wonderful." Right. Gulp. "We did it here you know." "What, at the Public?" "Yes. Right here. On this very stage."

Jonathan Cake (as Coriolanus) and Mo Sesay (as Aufidius) at the Globe Theatre, London in 2006

I'm in a cafe, feeling depressed at the virtue of my relentlessly healthy lunch and how all my gym visits seem unable to turn me back into a young man, when I start reading about the 75th anniversary of D-Day. John Eden, 94, was a 19-year-old boy in the 12th Battalion of the Devonshire Regiment. "Don't forget," I read, "I was a terrified little lad."

Shakespeare is forensically precise about Coriolanus's first experience of violence. "To a cruel war I sent him," says Volumnia, his mother. Coriolanus was 16. He met Tarquin, the fearsome Roman rebel king, and Tarquin, Shakespeare painstakingly enumerates, stabbed him seven times in the body. Seven times. I think of the 16-year-old son of the friends I'm staying with in Brooklyn and shudder.

So many of the D-Day survivors recall that first encounter with the extreme trauma of violence as a kind of stopped clock; that the rest of their lives have been lived with its constant and inescapable memory. I feel for the first time a kind of release from my concern about my age and fitness to play this part. If a part of him froze at 16, so much of his behaviour makes sense to me. Moody, instinctively rebellious, devoted to and simultaneously at war with his mother, unswervingly idealistic, as suspicious of phonies as a kind of weaponised Holden Caulfield. When his mother and friends are urging him to compromise, to play the obsequious politician and beg the people's forgiveness, Coriolanus, hurt, confused and betrayed, erupts with words that sound like any modern teenager:

> "I will not do it,
> Lest I surcease to honour _mine own truth..._"
> [my emphasis]

So much of what we now know as post-traumatic stress disorder is in Shakespeare's depiction of this man, including, as the _Publication Manual of the American Psychological Association_ describes it, anhedonia: the inability to experience pleasure. Maybe it doesn't matter that I'm 50 if inside he's a broken 16-year-old, his development savagely arrested, relentlessly trying – and failing – to cover it up.

13 JULY

TECHNICAL REHEARSAL, DELACORTE THEATER NEW YORK CITY

It's tech week, when a production moves into the theatre and goes through the often painful – and painfully slow – business of adding lights, sound, costumes, props, stage machinery – all a play's moving parts – to what the actors have rehearsed. We're stuck on a scene that has been a stone in our collective Birkenstocks for six weeks now: Act 3, scene 1. We all know why. It's bloody hard. It's one of Shakespeare's extraordinary "super scenes", immensely long, beginning in one state and ending a metaphorical thousand miles away, with the earth of relationships, status and narrative scorched in between.

It starts with a triumphant Coriolanus, fresh from his

extraordinary deeds at the battle of Corioles, on the verge of being crowned Consul of Rome, the president of this fledgling society. But, as so often in these great plays, the scene takes a sharp turn. Offstage, the Tribunes of the people, shop stewards of plebeian interests, have fomented an uprising against their new consul. Coriolanus launches into bitter invective against these two scheming upstarts, their new and disruptive power, whereupon the people of Rome storm the stage and an unholy riot breaks out. The Tribunes sentence him to death, Coriolanus wants to fight the lot of them right there and then:

> "No, I'll die here!
> There's some among you have beheld me fighting:
> Come, try upon yourselves what you have seen me."

The riot is beaten back out of the Capitol, Coriolanus is finally persuaded to sheathe his sword and the play has tipped into open civil war between him and, well, everyone.

We're really only supposed to be rehearsing sound cues but instead, despite the heat of the midday sun, we're in full riot mode, desperately trying to crack the code of how to have 30 people onstage screaming while still allowing the dialogue to be heard and the protagonists to be seen, how to fight whilst keeping everyone safe and most importantly, how to convey the genuine sense of it all kicking off while keeping it all simultaneously under control.

Another challenge is the extreme mutability of the mob in this play. One moment they adore Coriolanus, the next they're baying for his blood. This can seem like lazy writing on Shakespeare's part, until we realise it is just the opposite: it's an acute understanding of crowd dynamics and the way collective feelings, positive or negative, can reverse direction in an instant, like a forest fire in a changing wind.

These great plays, Peter Brook once said, are like planets: they orbit around us, moving closer to us depending on our current preoccupations. If social media is more a modern obsession than a preoccupation then this play feels more like an asteroid hurtling towards us than a gently orbiting planet. With this play Shakespeare basically wrote the handbook for the dynamics of every Twitter pile-on we've ever seen.

I sit down on one of the burnt-out oil drums on the set. Bad idea. It's well over a hundred degrees in Central Park and the dark metal has absorbed the heat of the sun. A scorched arse is pushing the burning relevance of the design concept a touch too far. Mindful of the fact that Coriolanus, perhaps the hardest man in all classical drama, should suck it up, I stifle my desire to cry, wander under an awning and lower myself gingerly next to the cooling agent that is James Shapiro.

Shapiro is a genius and the perfect man to see when your arse is scorched and your patience frayed. He's the Public Theater's dramaturg, resident Shakespeare scholar, a professor at Columbia University, author of some of the most insightful books on the plays and their author. He has forgotten more about Coriolanus than any of us will ever know.

"Did you know you're one of only a few actors in history to play this part twice?" Really? Who are the others. "Charles Kemble." Right. "Laurence Olivier." Got it. I'm not sure whether my arse is soothed or now has more complicated issues. "You're gonna be great" Jim says quietly. I take another sip of Gatorade, an extra slather of sunscreen and say to the grinning rioters, huddled in the shade of the rusted battlements of Rome: "All right you common cry of curs, who wants some?"

DELACORTE THEATER
NEW YORK CITY

"**G**ood evening. I'm Kate Burton and welcome to the Delacorte Theater." It's the first preview, the first public show. There are two thousand people out there. Kate, who plays my mother, Volumnia, does the introductory recorded message to the audience. I'm jogging from foot to foot and trying not to think about her dad. Richard was a pretty good Coriolanus. Only played it once, though; lightweight. Just as I'm trying to block out these thoughts, three little furry heads poke out from a gap in the side stage. Baby raccoons. They give me a coolly appraising look, not unlike what I'm expecting from the New York City punters who've queued all day for these tickets, then shimmy out of the scenery and make off into Central Park.

> "So, now the gates are ope: now prove good seconds:
> 'Tis for the followers fortune widens them,
> Not for the fliers: mark me and DO THE
> LIIIIIKE!"

The last three words are as bloodthirsty a rallying cry as I can muster and I turn and sprint through the open gates of Corioles, being careful to rapidly decelerate as

I get to the vertiginous stairs that lead down the back of the Delacorte looking out over Central Park's stately Belvedere Castle. Some small children and an elderly woman are feeding turtles in the pond and vigorously waving at me, delighted by the free peek backstage.

There's no time to wave back as I have seconds to stand in a child's paddling pool and have a bucket of fake blood poured over me before I'm back on to slaughter more character actors. I'm in the paddling pool, braced for the deluge of unctuously sweet, gooey gore to be poured. I'm a big unit and we need a lot of blood to cover me entirely, hence the paddling pool to catch it all. But there's no deluge. Just some agitated whispering.

What? Quick, pour the bloody blood! What? What are you whispering?! I've got to be back on in ten seconds and Shakespeare is very clear: "From face to foot he was a thing of blood." "Jonny, five seconds until you're back on," whispers the stage manager.

The whispering stops, the bucket is raised and... a small dribble of blood parts my hair. "Is that all? Where's the rest?" I hiss as I scramble up the stairs. The paddling pool attendants look sad and point to a nearby crime scene: macabre little bloodstained paw prints leading into the bushes. "The raccoons ate it all."

8 AUGUST

DELACORTE THEATER
NEW YORK CITY

I've finished the vocal warm-up, the physical warm-up and the fight call. I'm feeling more than usually keyed up tonight because the real Volumnia, my mother,

is here from England and in the house. As I make my
way back to the dressing rooms, from out of the clearest
of skies, a thunderclap and a sudden deluge of tropical
summer rain. Thus begins a strange limbo state peculiar to
this theatre, the state of not knowing if tonight you'll be
a tragic hero until midnight, or some guy wandering out
of Central Park looking for pizza at about 9.15pm. We can
hold for the weather to clear until about 9pm, when stage
and company management have to definitively tell the
soggy punters if their patience will be rewarded.

But, perhaps inspired by the war-child spirit of Margaret
Cake, who at the age of 86 sits drenched through the entire
night without an umbrella to shield her, we play on. And
it's a magical evening as the gentle cloud of rain, silver in
the stage lights, makes the action into a kind of Japanese
lithograph of *Blade Runner*.

The heat of Coriolanus's exertions make me steam
like a prize Friesian and, as I'm being hacked to pieces at
the play's climax by an angry mob of Volscians, the gods,
like a passionate New York audience keen to show their
feelings, perform a demented lightshow of an electrical
storm over Manhattan.

10 AUGUST

DELACORTE THEATER
NEW YORK CITY

It's our penultimate night. To mark the occasion we
have a pre-show speech from the grandest of the
many political fromages that have glommed on to
this free civic ritual: Chuck Schumer, Senate Minority
Leader and daddy of the Democratic Party. I'm doing my

antsy pre-show jog from foot to foot, hoping to hell that Chuck, a man I've admired for his no-bullshit attitude to Republican corruption and inequity, doesn't overstay his welcome when I hear the dread words: "So this is a play about a tyrant."

And I'm angry for a minute. Angry that he isn't enquiring or interested enough to read past the Wikipedia entry for this play. Angry that he's made my already tricky job – to defend and plead for this difficult, messy human being's humanity – ten times harder by condemning him with this lazy description. Angry that he wants to reduce Shakespeare's infinite complexity to fit a lazy soundbite. "So," Chuck continues, "does that kind of leader sound familiar to anybody?" I fantasise about introducing him at his next rally with a glib and reductive characterisation: "Don't forget folks, all politicians are lazy-minded, self-interested charlatans. Here he is, ladies and gentlemen – Chuck Schumer!"

But it doesn't matter because something's been going on during the run of this play that has been fascinating: a New York audience has been introduced to this play – and they dig it. It's like presenting a lost Shakespeare, a new play, virgin ground. And these fresh tracks we've made in the snow have felt clear and crisp. They seem, to these audiences, to lead somewhere.

Maybe the play has fallen into disuse in America because of its thorny political reputation, co-opted repeatedly throughout the 400 years of its history by Left and Right and still defying categorisation or an easy understanding of where Shakespeare's sympathies lay. Or whether it's because Coriolanus is most decidedly an anti-hero, difficult to love: an absurdly brave and principled man, incapable, unlike most politicians, of telling a lie; but also incapable of imagining people less brave and principled than him and condemning them utterly for being so. Or because, arriving at the final tragedy he would write, Shakespeare all but dispensed with glimpses into the soul through soliloquy or direct address to the audience.

Hamlet, as the brilliant scholar Emma Smith tells us, is constantly saying: "Oh you have no idea what it's like to be me!" And the audience keeps thinking: "Yes, yes we do! Because you keep telling us!" By the time Shakespeare gets to Coriolanus he is achieving an effect that has long since become Screenwriting 101: show, don't tell. We view this man almost totally from the outside, not from within. Maybe that is why the play has acquired the reputation, like its war-damaged protagonist, of being cold, uncommunicative, locked down.

But that's not what the audiences at the Delacorte seem to feel. Night after night, something seeps through the darkness and heat of the summer night, from stage to audience and back again: the joy of comprehension. Quite simply, they're getting it. So whatever Chuck Schumer sets up in an audience's mind, the play will do tonight what the play has been doing every night: connecting. Washing away the certainty of labels we start off with ("tyrant", "hero", "tragic", "comic") into something far more interesting and strange, both simultaneously hard to grasp and somehow familiar, inevitable. The laughter and the silence that accompanies the play is the audience recognising something they can truly understand: not just the 400-year-old language made explicable, but situations, characters, nuances from our common human experience. And even more, something all human beings can understand: the sense of something bad, something awful and inevitable coming to someone from way, way back. Events, circumstances, character; building, like tropical summer heat, into the inevitable cloudburst. The momentum of tragedy.

This is what Shakespeare can still do. I'm struck by the joy, the privilege, to be part of delivering an obscure but wonderfully urgent time capsule of human connection to this wild and beautiful corner of Central Park.

The Senator from New York/warm-up man leaves the stage. A small boy runs on, finds a rock, hides. A bunch of scrawny refugees from some kind of ecological nightmare take the stage, carrying clubs, iron bars. The kid throws the rock at them, misses, it clangs on the burnt-out metal around them. The boy, who will turn out to be Young Martius, Coriolanus's son, runs off. But the missile has punctured the mob's courage and they suddenly, urgently, need to talk. To move from action to language. And to lay out the inescapable emergency of this play:

"Before we proceed any further, hear me speak."

"Speak, speak!"

"You are all resolved rather to die than to famish?"

Backstage, my sense of Schumer failure recedes and I'm in. And I feel like the audience is too.

11 AUGUST

FINAL PERFORMANCE, DELACORTE THEATER
NEW YORK CITY

I t's the intermission. I come back into the dressing room and sit on the floor. Despite the fact that I take the world's fastest shower during the first half I can still feel the fake blood in my nostrils and ears. My clothes are drenched with sweat. Coriolanus has just been banished. He refuses to accept the city's power over him ("I banish YOU!") and has stalked off into "a world elsewhere". As he goes, someone cries:

"The people's enemy is gone, is gone!"

And like the crowd at Trump rallies crying "Lock her up!", the mob begin to chant:

"It. Shall. Be. So! It. Shall. Be. So!"

I look around the dressing room. Titus Lartius's station is as neat as a new pin. Tullus Aufidius's is the same, save for an industrial-sized tub of nuts to keep his warlord proteins high. Mine looks like Grey Gardens: earplugs, chilli flakes (to gargle with, old opera singer trick), alcohol rub and pads cut from a yoga mat for the pull-up bar near the theatre, a CBD stick for my dodgy shoulder, contact lenses, ginseng, a jar of instant espresso, numerous takeaway food boxes, critical essays, dead flowers. Like a homeless person's car, it's been the only place, mentally, I've had to live for the last six weeks. I think of clearing it all up at the end of this evening, throwing most of it

The Public Theater, Central Park, New York

away and returning to... what? California, domesticity, the school run, my intense and ongoing relationship with the dishwasher, whatever's next. All good and vital things.

I think I'll never play a part this hard, or this wonderful, again. And I feel, once more, the mad disorientation of the theatre actor: repeating and repeating the impossible task (like Beckett's famous line from *Worstward Ho*: "Try again. Fail again. Fail better."), making your body and mind dependent on the adrenalised state of the impossible task. And then abandoning the impossible task, never to repeat it. Your efforts existing entirely in the world of memory, like some nightly Burning Man. If these great plays are planets, in Peter Brook's phrase, then to me they seem more like dreams. Unreliable, disturbing, truer than life, entirely personal, entirely universal. And designed to be woken from.

I haul myself off the floor for the final time and go out to face my exile. ◖.

REBRAND

MILLENNIAL LIVING, EPISODE 2

IN THE VICIOUSLY COMPETITIVE CULINARY LANDSCAPE OF EVER-MORE-TRENDY FOODS, 'DELI JELLY' WAS CREATED WITH THE BOLD ASPIRATION OF, IN THE WORDS OF ONE OF THE CREATORS JOE, 'MAKING JELLY COOL AGAIN,' AND 'MAKING, LIKE, BILLIONS OF POUNDS'

Deli JELLY SPOTTED DICK

BUT IT WAS NOT TO BE. A DISASTER AT THE LAUNCH PARTY HAD DRAWN A SIGNIFICANT AMOUNT OF PRESS AND SUBSEQUENTLY GREATER INVESTIGATION INTO THE PRODUCT ITSELF. IT SEEMED PEOPLE WERE TAKING ISSUE WITH THE FLAVOUR, TEXTURE, INGREDIENTS AND STRANGE CHEMICAL AND MATERIAL PROPERTIES OF THE JELLY, ALTHOUGH ACCORDING TO CREATOR JOSH IT WAS 'REALLY AN IMAGE PROBLEM.'

Daily News

DIANA: 22 Years after her death we ask what she would have thought of Brexit, healing crystals, Richard Madden, dry shampoo and those weird toe trainers
PAGES 10-40

WATERFALL OF GOO
· Neon flames before Dalston building coated in a strange slime.
· Pigeons are now flocking to feast on the goo.

AREA DECLARED BIOHAZARD

IN AN EFFORT TO REVAMP THE BUSINESS JOSH HELD A SERIES OF CRISIS CONTROL MEETINGS IN OUR LIVING ROOM, THE LATEST OF WHICH EMMA AND I HAD BEEN INVITED TO. EMMA WAS PARTICULARLY INCENTIVISED BY THE FACT THAT SELLING THE JELLY WOULD GET RID OF ALL THE BOXES IN OUR FLAT.
Do the boxes have to be in the hallway? Why did you move them out of here? They're blocking the door to my bedroom.
Yeah well I noticed you tried to stack them behind the sofa and Kyle's painting is still pretty wet - you could damage it.
And what a tragedy that would be.

But we could tap into the whole artisan gin thing. You know, sprigs of rosemary, a few berries - why not some cubes of spotted dick jelly in there?
Jelly GIN HOUSE
I think the problem is that all cocktails are significantly improved by omitting it as an ingredient.
What about if the jelly was part of something new? The next fusion dessert like the cronut? Part of a cake or a muffin?

Yeah we don't serve that mainstream Mr Whippy crap, but how do you fancy a cone of elastic matter with an ambiguous flavour?
ICE CREAM

No can do - it also responds badly to the cold. Can't even really be refrigerated. Goes crunchy. Not sure why.
Surely there's a point to be made in the fact it's totally veggie...?
What, no gelatin?

I used moss – easy to source. Blended it up and it made a sort of binding agent. It's also really protein heavy because of all the powdered egg
TESCO
TESCO
Could it be a post-gym snack? Instead of a protein shake you have a protein jelly.
Yeah so I know it seems kind of paradoxical that jelly will make you stacked but it's like protein heavy weirdly firm stuff – powdered egg and like a moss goop all about those macros or whatever
JellyFIT
YUM! NOW! FIT! WOW!
Huh?
Dude, what aren't you getting? Just buy some.

I think the problem is that the flavour and texture are bad. Like, I can't really think of any person who would voluntarily eat it in any context.

NEW **Gourmet PET FOOD**

DELI JELLY IS A PREMIUM PET FOOD FOR THE SPECIAL FLUFFY, FEATHERED OR SCALED FRIEND IN YOUR LIFE!

IT'S A TOTALLY VEGETARIAN PRODUCT, LOVINGLY CRAFTED BY OUR FOUNDERS WHO WERE DEFINITELY MOTIVATED BY A LOVE FOR ANIMALS AND A DESIRE TO PROVIDE A GREEN ALTERNATIVE TO TRADITIONAL MEAT-BASED PET FOODS!

ARE YOU MORALLY AND ENVIRONMENTALLY CONSCIOUS? PROVE IT BY BUYING OUR PRODUCT!

TO BE CONTINUED...

A traveller in space

Organising 90s raves and The Big Chill festival led *Katrina Larkin* to co-found Fora, a Tortoise partner and a company bringing a sense of community and inspiration to the modern workplace

Portrait by Charlie Clift

When you hit a landmark birthday like 50 it's natural to take stock. Having done so, it now feels inevitable to me that my life-path would lead to the challenge of co-creating a community-based business such as Fora.

I grew up in an incredibly creative house in north London; my mother is a painter and my father was an internationally renowned luthier – crafting guitars and basses. They approached their work with great passion and discipline, always prepared to take an untrodden path in pursuit of their art. From the earliest age, their example has informed the way I work too.

My father had taught at St Anthony's School in Hampstead, which was not just a job but a community of free-thinking, spirited teachers led by the maverick Tim Patton. Many a weekend I was to be found tagging along with a troupe of miming schoolboys through Hampstead. It was an idyllic childhood, but it changed suddenly in 1977, partly due to the publication of *The Complete Book of Self-Sufficiency*.

My dad bought the guide and then a trailer into which all our worldly possessions were loaded. He announced that we would be moving to the west coast of Ireland, to the remote location where

we had holidayed with Tim each summer. For an eight-year-old this was devastating news. In the late 70s, County Kerry and Hampstead were worlds apart. Republican sentiment in Kerry was high and tensions were evident daily; my mother even feared revealing her English accent. At primary school the headmaster would often make me stand at the back of the class until I could speak in an accent he understood. On my first day at secondary school the nuns sat me next to the daughter of a well-known Republican gunrunner.

This is not a sob story, however. Whilst my world had been completely disrupted, I quickly learnt to adapt – and in many ways my experience in Kerry forged the mindset and world view that would direct the course of my life. It embedded within me the impulse to embrace people with different perspectives and attitudes. I learnt the true importance of culture and how opening up to change, however challenging, could bring the richest experiences, insights and a fuller picture of the world. Above all, it opened my eyes and gave me the strength to explore all opportunities.

While this remote corner of Ireland might have seemed lonely and isolated, my parents were visited by a steady stream of musicians and fellow artists and I embraced the talents and ideas each of these guests brought with them. Outside of these visitors, my companions were books, my dad's seemingly limitless record collection and the Dave Fanning radio show. Little did I know at the time that this daily consumption of culture would be an education that prepared me for life far better than anything I learnt formally.

I returned to London in 1990, a tumultuous year of poll tax riots and stark social divisions. Like many others I found my refuge in music and the orbital rave scene. I started going to (and occasionally co-organising) dance parties like Tribal Gathering, Club Together and Rhythm Method. I loved them, but at the same time I could also see the limitations of the nascent dance formula. While music brought people together, just as it had in my parents' home throughout my childhood, the environment was so noisy and crowded there was very little exchange of ideas. Basically, you went to dance; people couldn't talk to each other.

Someone who shared this view was Pete Lawrence. Together we founded The Big Chill festival, driven by a desire to see culture and conversation go hand in hand. The first one was at London's Union Chapel in February 1994. We had about £45 in our back pockets and my flatmate Emma and I stayed up all night baking

The Reading Room

I mentioned how much music means to me, how it can set my moods and help my thinking, and the wall here reflects just some of my tastes. And these records are not just ornamental; they are not just beautiful to look at. I, or any of our residents, can take these albums down and play them. Some of the artists have been here too. But it's not just my music, it's a record collection and we all like to look through other people's collections, don't we?

People come here to talk, rest, meditate, read poetry, play board games and listen to music.

cakes. I collected old mattresses from skips to give people something to sit on. But people came. And they kept coming – about a thousand every Sunday – to a place where they could listen to artists like Orbital, but could also talk, eat, learn or just hang out. Then the next year we went to Llanthony in Wales and took 700 friends with us. The police came too, but everything was peaceful and we knew we had something special.

For a golden decade I talked my way around London, persuading the great and the good, the artists, the institutions, the innovators, to come together in a field or two. Soon much more than a festival, The Big Chill quickly evolved into a year-round community of like-minded, open-hearted, culturally inquisitive "chillers" for whom the festival was the highlight of the year. And the community grew and grew. From hundreds in '94, we quickly grew to tens of thousands – the maximum we felt we could sustain without losing the magic.

Innovation was at the heart of The Big Chill. Just as my parents had forged their own path in search of their creative goals, I introduced elements that were novelties in the 90s but have since become mainstream. At the dawn of the digital age we were the first festival to use the internet to bring our audience together when many of our rivals

The Fora app
Almost all my working life is here. On this app I can roam our rooms, see what meetings I am supposed to attend, what Fora events will inspire me the most and carry out all my conversations with Enrico and other members of the team across all the Fora spaces. I can even bother the concierge by ringing his bell.

still relied on fliers, phone lines and wild goose chases around the M25. Film and technology tents, street food and wellness zones were unheard of then but we believed we could offer something genuinely different and, from brain machines to gong meditation, our audience loved it.

By the time I left The Big Chill in 2009 we had taken our festivals all over the world, to Australia, New Zealand, Japan and across Europe – a marvellous travelling circus for new ideas and platforms, constantly experimenting with art and technology. The artists who appeared with us included Leonard Cohen, David Byrne (I had promised myself his appearance for my 40th!), Lily Allen, Massive Attack and Biosphere. But beyond the headliners, we covered everything from tech workshops to spoken word performances. It was the innovative partnerships, installations and commissions that I'm most proud of.

I won't pretend that leaving The Big Chill behind was easy. I knew it would certainly be a big first act to follow. I was wandering one day through Camden Lock, marvelling at the timeworn cobbled market area packed with stalls, and realised that there were a wealth of similarities between the neighbourhood and the festival world. And then I had one of those chance meetings where serendipity can send life in a new direction. I was introduced to Camden Lock's new owners, Brockton Capital, and given the opportunity to work with them to evolve the fabric and community of the beloved market. I knew I could take the skills I'd honed at The Big Chill and transfer them.

After a year, Brockton sold Camden Lock to a new owner who also owned all the other markets within Camden, and the challenge expanded again into an entire ecosystem, uniting commerce, culture and community. In among this burgeoning district we decided to open a co-working space, which would be tailored to meet the needs of a new breed of worker and company. It reflected a rapidly emerging trend in the workplace and it provided the confidence for me to enter my next project. I knew there was a new way for people to form communities that could elevate the grey sterility of the traditional office into a hotbed of energy and positivity.

As I had learnt throughout my childhood and have practised throughout my career to date, bringing people together and inspiring them takes a special combination of elements. If the right kind of environment is nurtured, creativity thrives and ideas flow. So, by the time Enrico Sanna and

The Fora podcast studios in Soho We have three of them, all glass-fronted so people can see what is going on, feel the excitement. Most podcasts are made in places that look like bedsit kitchens with egg boxes stuck on the walls. Not ours!

The Flotation Tanks
Strictly speaking this belongs to one of our partners, 3Tribes wellness studio. I'm going there this evening. I will lie there, alone, in the dark, and miraculously my mind will clear. The first time I tried it I thought I would find it claustrophobic and have to leave but the hour flew by. I had switched off. It was wonderful.

I co-founded Fora I knew what we were going to do. I'd learned that people wanted to be treated with respect and be given the space to concentrate on their work, but they also wanted to be inspired and to turn their ideas into reality. After all, we spend more time with our work colleagues than we do with family and friends. We wanted to give our residents a space which is much more than just a place to work.

Fora has already grown to ten locations and our community is expanding rapidly too, as we are joined by wonderful talents like the people at Tortoise. They are a great example of how we are striving to create something inspirational in each location, by helping to bring people together, to share ideas and to maximise our individual productivity – while enjoying life to the full. I love the ThinkIns – what could be better for a meeting place like us? We are offering all our residents access to news they can trust and rely upon. It's a perfect fit. ◠.